Funny Cars

DEDICATION

To the great Creightons—Bob and Ruth

First published in 2000 by MBI Publishing Company, 729 Prospect Avenue, PO Box 1, Osceola, WI 54020-0001 USA

MBI Publishing Company books are also available at discounts in bulk quantity for industrial or sales-promotional use. For details write to Special Sales Manager at Motorbooks International Wholesalers & Distributors, 729 Prospect Avenue, PO Box 1, Osceola, WI 54020-0001 USA.

Library of Congress Cataloging-in-Publication Data
Genat, Robert
     Funny cars / Robert Genat.
       p.cm.
     Includes index.
     ISBN 0-7603-0795-4 (pbk.)
        1. Funny cars. I. Title.

TL236.23 .G45 2000
629.228 – dc21

On the front cover: The wildest and woolliest ride in all of drag racing is in the seat of a nitro-burning Funny Car. A Funny Car accelerates to 100 miles per hour in less than one second and can reach speeds in excess of 324 miles per hour at the finish line. Dean Skuza, at the wheel of the Matco Tools Dodge Avenger, starts one of his patented prolonged burnouts.

On the frontispiece: The only gauge in a Funny Car is an oil pressure gauge. Mounted directly in front of the driver, it's there to let him know if the engine is healthy when it's fired up.

On the title page: One of the last things the driver does when staging a Funny Car is to turn on the fuel pumps. This is done from the driver's seat with a lever control. This is often called "doubling up." The extra load on the engine from the fuel pumps causes the idle rpm to drop slightly.

On the back cover: In addition to winning multiple world championships, John Force has become a fan favorite. His lengthy burnouts bring the crowd to its feet, and his TV interviews have the intensity of a Gatling gun. Each time he pulls his Castrol Funny Car to the line, fans know they are going to get their money's worth. Hidden under the clouds of tire smoke and blustery dialogue is one of the world's best Funny Car drivers and race team owners.

Edited by Keith Mathiowetz
Designed by Eric Aurand

Printed in China

CONTENTS

ACKNOWLEDGMENTS

While gathering information for this book, I had the privilege of talking to some of the greats, past and present, of the Funny Car world. The following men were all extremely helpful by passing on their history in the sport, technical information on what makes a Funny Car tick, and what it's like to sit in the driver seat of a Funny Car at 300 miles per hour. Thanks to "Dyno" Don Nicholson, Charlie DiBari, John Buttera, John Force, Ed "The Ace" McCulloch, Don "The Snake" Prudhomme, Ron Capps, Lance Larson, Dean Skuza, Austin Coil, Bernie Fedderly, Tony Pedregon, and Don Schumacher.

Thanks must also go out to the crews of John Force's Castrol and Castrol Syntec Funny Cars, Don Prudhomme Racing's Copenhagen/American Tobacco Companies Funny Car, and Dean Skuza's Matco Tools Funny Car. Thank you for your patience in allowing me to invade your space while at the track, and for answering my questions.

At the NHRA, I'd like to thank Rick Stewart, Steve Gibbs, and Greg Sharp. Getting a starting line photo pass for an NHRA event at Pomona is more difficult than getting a seat next to Cher at the Oscars. A special thanks must go out to Lisa Guth for getting me on the list.

Thanks to the following for their help: Joe McCaron, Pamela Przywara at the Ford Archives, Judy Stropus at JVS Enterprises, Dave Clinton at Darton International, John Logghe at Logghe Stamping, Dave Densmore at Denswood Sports Marketing, and a special thanks to one of the nation's top motorsports announcers, Steve Evans. Thanks to the following photographers for their contribution of historical photos to this book: Ron Lewis, Curt Stimpson, Charles Krasner, Joe Veraldi, Larry Davis, Jere Alhadeff; and to Tom West for his excellent cutaway illustration.

—*Robert Genat*

6

INTRODUCTION

In the summer of 1965, I took my 1957 Chevy to Detroit Dragway. Because of school, work, and the time it took to build my car, it had been almost a year since I'd been to the strip. After going through tech inspection, getting classified, and un-corking the exhaust, I rolled into the staging lanes to wait my turn to run. While sitting in my car, I heard this apocalyptic roar going by in the staging lane next to me. It was the Ramchargers 1965 Dodge, and it was unlike any other Dodge I'd ever seen. It had injectors sticking out of the hood and the body had been moved back on the chassis. The big slicks on the back were pushed up near the rear edge of the door and the front wheels were a good foot forward of where they should have been. And the exhaust smell was strangely pungent. Modified super stockers like this were now called Funny Cars, for obvious reasons. Things had definitely changed since the last time I'd been to the strip.

The relatively new sport of drag racing was changing daily in the 1960s and the Funny Car was at the leading edge of those changes. In the 1970s, the cars and the audience were getting more outrageous. On the West Coast, where drag-sters were once king, Funny Car shows were now the big draw. Midwest Super Stock events were re-placed with Funny Car match races. Staunch drag-ster drivers, who a few years earlier looked down their collective noses at Funny Cars, were now making the switch. NHRA gave the Funny Car re-spectability in 1969, when a Funny Car class was officially added to national event eliminations.

New drag-racing heroes, who were not re-cruited from the dragster side, also emerged from the Funny Car ranks. This new breed proved to be as sexy as the cars they raced. To be a top com-petitor, the Funny Car driver had to have person-ality, along with a great deal of courage. The cars and the drivers were unpredictable and volatile. Crafty promoters made the most of these person-alities in a way that could be best compared to today's professional wrestling.

Today, Funny Cars are one of the highlights of any NHRA national event. The Top Fuel drag-sters may be quicker and faster, but they don't hold the crowd's attention like an unpredictable pair of Funny Cars. As they idle at the starting line, each pipe creating the report of a 12-gauge shotgun blast, it's hard to believe that within five seconds that car will be a quarter-mile from the starting line. When the Christmas tree flashes green, all hell breaks loose! The noise is deafening and the ground shakes. The easiest way to de-scribe the violence at the start of a Funny Car race is to compare it to an explosion. If you're down near the starting line, the concussion is visceral. Even veteran drivers are amazed by this when they stand at the starting line, watching other competitors. Within one second of the start, a Funny Car has already reached a speed of 100 miles per hour. A modern Funny Car race may be a 300-mile per hour side-by-side duel decided by inches at the finish line, or it might be a "pedal-fest" where both cars smoke the tires the entire length of the track with each driver repeatedly stabbing the throttle to allow the tires to get a bite. Funny Car runs are always exciting—and always unpredictable.

Following the lead of Nicholson's ground-breaking Mercury Comet, most Funny Cars preserved the external dimensions of the original production car body. In the late 1960s, Mickey Thompson was racing cars for Ford Motor Company. This 1970 Mustang Mach 1, which was built in his shop, carried the same beautiful proportions as a production Mach 1.

THE BIRTH OF THE FUNNY CAR

No one knows for sure how the name Funny Car came about. Most of us believe that it was a track announcer who, after looking at one of the altered wheelbase cars, found that the only way to describe the unusual configuration was to call it a "funny car." The name stuck.

The first altered wheelbase cars, later to be known as Funny Cars, were products of Chrysler's engineering department. In the dead of the winter of 1964–1965, Chrysler flew all of its factory-sponsored teams to Detroit to attend a clinic on Chrysler's 1965 model Super Stock and A/FX cars. The names of those attending read like a Who's Who of future drag-racing legends. From the West Coast came Butch Leal, H.L. Shahan, Tom Grove, and Dick Landy. Traveling from the East Coast were Bud Faubel, Dave Strickler, and the team of Ronnie Sox and Buddy Martin. Local Detroit racers, Roger Lindamood, Jim Thorton, and Al Eckstrand, rounded out the attendees. There, in Chrysler's Skunk Works, these gentlemen were shown the latest Dodge and Plymouth race cars.

The most noteworthy cars in that shop were the altered wheelbase models. The altered wheelbase cars looked as though the body had been shifted rearward over the chassis. To accomplish the alteration, both the front and rear suspensions were modified. The rear axle was moved forward 15 inches, placing the rear wheel just rear of the door opening. The front wheels were moved forward 10 inches, requiring a special cross-member.

In 1965, Chrysler's engineers upped the ante in the manufacturer's drag-racing poker game when they released their altered wheelbase cars. Both Dodge and Plymouth models were built and delivered to the factory teams. Hemi engines were initially equipped with dual quads, but most teams quickly switched to fuel injection. Curt Stimpson

Stainless steel was chosen for light weight and strength. The bodies of these cars were constructed out of sheet stock that was thinner than on the production versions. Fiberglass doors, hood, front fenders, deck lid, and instrument panel were built for Chrysler by Plaza Fiberglass Manufacturing in Dearborn, Michigan. The work done by Chrysler's engineers to reduce the weight of these cars paid off. The new Mopars weighed in at a svelte 2,500 pounds.

Ramcharger club member and Chrysler engineer Tom Hoover talked to the group about the latest revisions to the Hemi engine. New aluminum heads and a magnesium intake manifold were on the long list of improvements. Chrysler selected an Isky roller cam as standard equipment for the 1965 Hemi. With all the improvements, the Hemi was still rated at 425 horsepower at 6,000 rpm. (Estimates of true horsepower were between 500 and 600.)

Ford was not standing by, waiting for the Mopars to hit the strip. Ford embarked on a plan in which it would contract with a specialty shop to assemble its cars. One big change was the selection of a new platform. In 1964, the successful

Ford Motor Company was the first manufacturer with a contract to an outside firm for construction a drag-racing car. The Thunderbolt, built by Dearborn Steel Tubing, was based on the midsized Fairlane; it featured lightweight body panels and a 427 engine. Because of its limited production numbers, the Thunderbolts were relegated to the Factory Experimental class.

Thunderbolts had been built from the midsize "mom and pop" Fairlane. Yet the Fairlane did not have a performance image and its sales were not substantially boosted by its drag strip wins. The next year, Ford would put its drag strip emphasis on the sporty Mustang.

In 1965, Ford contracted to have the Holman & Moody shop in Charlotte, North Carolina, build its drag-race cars. For the 1965 season, NHRA set the minimum A/FX vehicle weight at 3,200 pounds. For the strip, the new Mustang was put on a strict diet with extensive use of fiberglass for hood, doors, and front fenders. These were added to a stock Mustang fastback body. The rear seat was removed and the glass windows were replaced with plexiglass. The rear wheel wells were enlarged to accept the massive 10.00x15 M&H Racemaster slicks that were mounted on 6-inch-wide American mags. The rear axle was moved forward 2 inches and special traction bars were added to the rear. To make room in the engine compartment for the large V-8, the spring towers were removed. Installed as a replacement for the coil spring was a flat leaf torsion bar. The interior was stripped of all unnecessary frills (radio, heater, and sound deadener) and a sturdy roll cage was installed.

Ford struggled to remain competitive against Mopar's free-breathing Hemi engine. Ford engineers had to do something, and do it quickly. They came up with their version of Chrysler's Hemi head, but they upped the ante by adding a single overhead camshaft to each side. Officially called the Single Overhead Cam (SOHC) 427, this engine was affectionately called a "Cammer" by Ford enthusiasts.

Ford started with the same reliable 427 high-riser block it had used the previous two years. Ford's engineers added a set of special hemispherical heads. The new hemi heads were beautifully designed,

each incorporating a SOHC. The cams were driven at half the crankshaft speed by a 6-foot chain drive. The advantage to the overhead cam was the elimination of the traditional valvetrain, which limited the engine's higher rpm range. Atop each head were two rocker shafts with roller cam followers. Ford's engineers used the experience they had with overhead cam engines from their Indy program to design this engine. Sitting atop the Cammer were a pair of Holley four-barrel carbs. A special duct system fed cool air from behind the Mustang's grille to the carbs. With the Cammer, Ford produced an engine that could rev—up to and over 8,000 rpm—as well as it could breathe. This design,

Ford's Thunderbolt looked like an ordinary sedan, except that the inside headlights had been converted into air intakes and a bubble was added to the hood. Powered by a dual-quad 427, it was a revolutionary car in its day.

In 1965, Ford contracted with the Holman & Moody race shop to build its drag-race cars. Instead of pumping horsepower into a frumpy Fairlane sedan, Ford selected the popular Mustang for modification. The exterior changes were subtle, with the bubble hood being the most obvious. Chrysler felt that Ford had violated the "spirit of competition" when it introduced the small Mustang to compete against the larger Dodges and Plymouths.

while bulky, was Ford's answer to Chrysler's Hemi in 1965.

At the season opening 1965 NHRA Winternationals, Bill Lawton won the A/FX class in his Cammer-powered Mustang with a run of 10.92 seconds and a top speed of 128.20. Later in 1965, Gas Rhonda, driving a Cammer-powered Mustang, set the A/FX record at 10.43 seconds with a speed of 134.73.

Chrysler debuted its gaggle of Super Stock and A/FX combatants at the 1965 American Hot Rod Association (AHRA) Winter Championships held in Scottsdale, Arizona, on January 29, 30, and 31. To differentiate itself from the NHRA, class designations for exotic factory stock cars were not labeled "factory experimental." Ultra/Stock (U/S) designated altered wheelbase cars with lightweight body components with a minimum weight of 3,000 pounds. Super/Stock (S/S) designated stock or 2 percent altered wheelbase cars that were equipped with lightweight body components. Super/Stock-1 (S/S-1) designated steel body standard wheelbase

Ford played its trump card under the hood of the 1965 Mustang with the built-for-drag-racing-only SOHC 427. The new Hemi-style heads were exceptionally free breathing, and the overhead cam allowed the engine to rev like a kitchen blender on high speed.

The Mercury Division had a few of its small Comets modified for drag racing in 1964 and 1965. Jack Chrisman was not content with the car as delivered, so he added a few modifications, including a supercharger, a drag chute, and a straight front axle. Ford Motor Company

cars. Both S/S and S/S-1 had a minimum weight of 3,200 pounds. "The Plymouth we took to the AHRA meet to run in the Super Stock class weighed 2,500 pounds when we got it," says Charlie DiBari, owner of the *Melrose Missile.* "We had to add weight, all behind the rear axle, to get up to the minimum." The Melrose Missile was the fastest S/S qualifier, with a time of 11.03 seconds. The fastest U/S qualifier was the team of Sox and Martin at 10.74 seconds.

The only Ford contender at the AHRA Winter Championships was Phil Bonner, who qualified a 427-powered 1964 Falcon in U/S at 10.83. Sitting on his trailer at this meet was his brand-new Cammer Mustang. Ford officials didn't want the, as yet, untried Mustang to run against the Mopars. Ford also felt that Chrysler hadn't kept within the spirit of the "rules" with its altered wheelbase race offerings. Top Stock Eliminator at the meet was Bud Faubel driving the Hemi Honker 1965 Dodge U/S. In the final run, he beat Al Eckstrand's Plymouth with an elapsed time of 10.96 seconds at 129.31 miles per hour.

Early season squabbling between Ford and Chrysler over the "legality" of their cars caused quite a bit of angst for track

The racing team of Sox & Martin raced one of the altered wheelbase Hemi Plymouths. To remain competitive in match races, Sox & Martin added Hilborn fuel injection and a small competition-style fuel tank to the grille. As the 1965 racing season progressed, the use of exotic fuels increased. Because of the extra horsepower being extracted from the Hemi, and due to the thin sheet metal from which they were constructed, Chrysler's altered wheelbase cars experienced some structural problems with the unitized bodies. Larry Davis

owners and competitors. A Ford versus Ford or Mopar versus Mopar meet had the drawing power of a cold bowl of soup. Ford was annoyed that Chrysler had radically altered the wheelbase of its factory experimental Dodges and Plymouths. Chrysler was upset because Ford used the smaller Mustang for its A/FX car instead of its midsize Fairlane. The anger escalated and Ford directed its racers not to race any car that would not be legal under NHRA A/FX rules. The altered wheelbase Mopars and a few independents running Chevys did not qualify as legal A/FX cars under NHRA rules. If a Ford factory

competitor were to race an altered wheelbase Mopar, the penalty was a recall of the race car, engines, and spare parts. Chrysler's penalty for an infraction was an end to support—no more free parts.

Running a factory race car meant that you had to follow factory rules. In an era before e-mail, FedEx, and fax machines, the only way to get a written message out quickly was by Western Union telegram. On May 11, 1965, H. Dale Reeker of Chrysler sent the following telegram to its race teams.

"You are to use gasoline only as fuel in your race car. Further suggest that you

Arnie "The Farmer" Beswick ran Pontiacs when GM was still involved in racing. When GM dropped out, Beswick ran a Mercury Comet, but he was never competitive. He abandoned the Comet and reworked his 1963 Tempest by severely altering the wheelbase. He was one of the few who raced GM products without factory support. Larry Davis

insist that your match race competitors burn gasoline only. Disregarding this rule will result in cancellation of our agreement with you."

On May 18, 1965, Reeker sent another telegram:

"I believe the wheelie situation is getting out of hand. It is dangerous and expensive in terms of car maintenance and parts breakage. Therefore I am requesting that all the factory A/FX cars refrain from doing wheel stands. Just tell the promoters that the factory won't let you do wheelies."

It's difficult to tell if Reeker ever set foot out of his corporate cubicle to get out

to the track. If he had, he would have found that life on the strip, where all that mattered was winning or losing, was a different environment from his Detroit office.

It didn't take long for the two main combatants to realize that there was too much to lose by fighting on paper and not on the track. Soon it was Mustang versus Dodge, or Plymouth versus Mustang. The few A/FX Mercury Comets built at Bill Stroppe's shop also got into the match race frenzy. Initially, the Comets were running with the biggest disadvantage because of their stock wheelbase. This soon changed when Don "Dyno"Nicholson moved the rear wheels of his Comet

In 1962, Gay Pontiac in Dickinson, Texas, sponsored its first race car, a Super Duty 421 Catalina, driven by the owner's son, Don Gay. His younger brother, Roy, is seen here driving the Gay Pontiac Funny Car, a modified 1965 Pontiac GTO. This early Funny Car featured a supercharged Pontiac engine and altered wheelbase with a beam front axle.

Like most early Funny Car drivers, Hubert Platt had risen from the Super Stock ranks. He ran this highly modified Mustang through 1966. It features the long nose and a fuel-injected 427 Cammer engine. Platt's truck was typical of those used in 1966 to transport a Funny Car to the strip. Larry Davis

forward 10 inches. Earlier in the year, the Golden Commandos team was the first to fit a Hemi Plymouth with Hilborn Fuel injection. It wasn't long before all the major Mopar teams were running fuel injection too. Nicholson added Hilborn injection to his Comet's Cammer engine. The Hilborn injectors were fitted to a manifold originally designed for Weber carburetors. Nicholson also removed the stock front suspension and added a Woody Gilmore straight front axle. Running on gas, Nicholson's Comet ran the quarter in 10.28 seconds at 134 miles per hour. With the addition of an exotic fuel blend,

Nicholson became the first Comet driver to run in the nines, when he ran a 9.91 at 137 miles per hour.

In November 1965, Chrysler realized that A/FX and match racing was out of step with the exposure it originally wanted from drag racing. The cars it was racing were no longer representative of the cars being sold in the dealerships. Chrysler sent a letter to its race teams explaining that the factory emphasis would once again be placed on the Super Stock class and not on exhibition or A/FX. Prompting this change was the imminent release of the Street Hemi. Chrysler also felt that the

Brothers Ron and Gene Logghe developed their part-time race car hobby into a business. They designed and built the chassis for several different types of race cars. When called upon by Mercury to build a chassis for its 1966 Funny Car, they built one similar to what they were building for altered coupes. This is the chassis for Nicholson's Eliminator I. It was a simple frame constructed from chrome-moly tubing and was fully sprung with coil-over shocks, front and rear. The driver seat was positioned in the center of the car, which made it hard to shift the four-speed transmission. Logghe collection escalating cost and safety implications of running a blown fuel-burning car would be excessive.

For the 1966 season, Chrysler offered 1965 Funny Car teams parts, machining expenses, and 10 cents per mile for travel. Chrysler also signed over the title to the car. One caveat was that the cars could run fuel, but no blowers. Chrysler competitors were instructed to refuse match races against any blown car. It was at this point that many of the Chrysler factory teams quit racing. Others who ran Chryslers decided to build all-out match race cars. In Dearborn, plans were in place to build a new series of Mustangs for 1966. These cars would be known as the "long nose" Mustangs because of their extended front fenders.

In the early and mid-1960s, Ron and Gene Logghe were highly respected Detroit area dragster chassis builders, building

In the late 1960s, Funny Cars came in all shapes and sizes, and were powered by different makes of engines. This Corvair, driven by Terry Hendrick, featured a Logghe chassis and a supercharged big-block Chevy engine. At that time, drag strip promoters were able to promote match races featuring Chevy versus Ford; and the fans actually saw a car with a Chevy engine race a car with a Ford engine. Before long, all Funny Cars were powered by the Chrysler Hemi engine. Logghe collection

In 1966, Don Nicholson's Mercury Comet Funny Car revolutionized drag racing. On the outside, Nicholson's car looked like a standard Mercury Comet. Under the flip-top fiberglass body was a race car chassis with a SOHC 427. Ford Motor Company

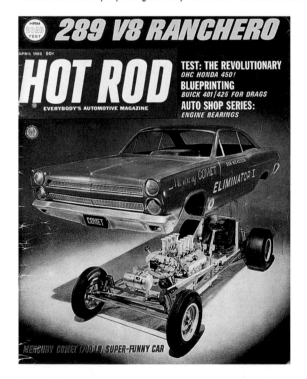

The introduction of Nicholson's unique Funny Car prompted Hot Rod magazine to feature it on the cover of its April 1966 issue. Out of the box, this car set records and a trend in Funny Car design that has persisted through today—the flip-top body. The nickname of "Floppers," commonly used for Funny Cars, was first given to this car.

dragsters for Connie Kalitta and Shirley Muldowney. Earlier, the brothers made their mark in the Midwest with an injected Chevy-powered dragster. The Logghe, Marsh, and Steffie *Giant Killer* weighed only 900 pounds with the driver. Because of its light weight and high-revving Chevy engine, it was capable of outrunning most blown Chrysler dragsters. What started out as a part-time hobby grew into a full-time business by 1965, supplying race car chassis and components to a wide range of competitors.

Leading the Mercury racing effort was Al Turner (who, because of his blustery ways, was called "Big Thunder" behind his back) under the direction of Mercury's Fran Hernandez. It was Turner who collaborated with the Logghe brothers for the chassis design on the 1966 Comet. Mercury's effort for 1966 was the most dramatic and innovative Funny Car yet. John Logghe, son of Gene, recalls, "Al Turner had this idea and came to Gene and Ron. They said, 'No problem, we can do it.' They came up with what is known

Mickey Thompson was one of the most prolific race car builders of the 1960s. Danny Ongias drove this 1969 Mach 1 for Thompson. Funny Car bodies in the 1960s were close replicas of the original cars and some, like this Mustang, even had grille and C-pillar emblems, side marker lights, and door handles (which went unused). This car also has an unusual, high-mounted rear wing. Ford Motor Company

The new world of Funny Cars was open to experimentation in design and construction. Most were built with a tube frame and covered by a fiberglass body shell. Mickey Thompson's 1970 Mach 1 was unique, because it was built with an aluminum monocoque chassis, similar to the open-wheel cars that Thompson ran at the Indianapolis 500. Nye Frank, one of the craftsmen who worked for Thompson, built this car. The grille is a production Mustang piece.

as the modern-day tubular chassis flip-top Funny Car. It was all done here." A set of drawings was made and then fixtures were built for the assembly of the side frames. "Back then," says John, "there was no CAD-CAM or anything like that—it was all seat-of-the-pants, and that's where these two guys were geniuses in their own right." Several off-the-shelf components were used on the cars the brothers built, like spindles, steering boxes, Heim joints, and axles. But just about everything else on that car was made in-house. The inventive brothers even turned their own bellhousings.

The plan was to build four cars, with the first one going to Don Nicholson. The

Thompson's 1970 Mach 1 was an innovative design that came in underweight for the class and ballast had to be added. Both Danny Ongias and Mike Van Sant drove this car, but it was not competitive and was quickly retired.

Because of the monocoque construction on Thompson's Mach 1, only a portion of the body was hinged at the rear. The large monocoque tub made servicing the engine, and access to the driver seat, difficult.

frame's main rails were constructed out of 1 1/2-inch-diameter chrome moly tubing. The roll cage was built out of a slightly beefier 1 7/8-inch-diameter chrome moly. The front axle was tubular, supported by a four-bar suspension with coil-over shocks. Coil-overs were also used in the rear with ladder bars. The 9-inch Ford rear end (4.11:1 ratio) was narrowed to keep the slicks within the wheel openings. The brake system consisted of disc units on the rear. The seating position was more in the back seat than in the front, and the seat was skewed slightly toward the center of the car.

The engine was the Cammer fitted with Hilborn fuel injectors. The compression ratio was dropped from its usual 12:1 to 10:1 to accommodate the expected 75 percent nitro mix. The engine also featured a Crane cam, Mallory Super-Mag ignition, and custom-made headers with 32-inch tubes that dumped into 12-inch long collectors. Before long, the headers were replaced with dragsterlike individual pipes. Initially, Nicholson's car was fitted with a T-10 four-speed with a Hurst shifter. Because of the position of the seat, the shifter ended up between Nicholson's legs. "We tried the four-speed, but it didn't work," says Nicholson. "I couldn't drive it with the shifter between my legs—we went right to the automatic." The Cammer was also a handful connected to a four-speed. The modified C6 transmissions were easier to drive and performed well.

Topping off the Logghe chassis was a custom-built 1966 Comet body. It was crafted out of fiberglass by Plastigage Corporation in Jackson, Michigan, with a Ford engineering styling model for the mold.

The body's total weight was 250 pounds, which included the 1/8-inch-thick plexiglass side windows and 3/8-inch-thick windshield and backlight. For reinforcement, five plywood bulkheads were installed with additional strength coming from a network of 1/2-inch tubes. Paul Shedlik of Taylor, Michigan, sprayed on the candy tangerine paint; the bumpers, grille, and headlights were sprayed silver. From a distance, it had the appearance of a factory stock Comet. On the side of Nicholson's car, in gold letters outlined in black, was the very appropriate name, *Eliminator I*. Mercury Comet was written conspicuously on the front fender. Eddie Schartman drove the Air Lift–sponsored *Air Lift Rattler*, Jack Chrisman ran the *GT-1*, which was sponsored by Kendall Oil, and the 1966 final car went to the team of Kenz and Leslie.

The one-piece Comet body was hinged at the rear, allowing it to open for access to the engine and driver seat. Up until the time this car was built, Funny Cars either had doors or the driver climbed in through the open side windows. While the Comet was designed for the driver to enter and exit through the missing driver-side window, most drivers climbed in and out with the body in the open position.

Mercury's newest race car design set the trend for the design of all future Funny Cars—a one-piece fiberglass body hinged in the rear. Because of the rear hinged opening, the Comets were soon dubbed "floppers" for the way the body flopped open and closed. These cars also immediately rewrote the record book by dropping into the eight-second range— cutting a full second off of the previous best Funny Car run.

Powering Mickey Thompson's 1970 Mach 1 was a supercharged Boss 429 engine. This engine, with its distinctive valve covers, was originally designed to compete against Chrysler's Hemis in NASCAR. Ford encouraged several factory drag racers to use the engine, but it was not as successful as the Cammer engine.

At the 1967 AHRA Winternational meet held at the Bee Line drag strip in Phoenix, Arizona, Nicholson bested the field by running an 8.26 elapsed time at 172.08 miles per hour. His competitor in the final run for Unlimited Stock Eliminator was Ed Schartman in another Comet.

The only way competitors could compete with the new Mercury Comet was to build a car in the same fashion or add a blower. Most did both. The new crop of cars no longer had the distorted wheelbase proportions of the 1965 models. They looked more like passenger cars with a race car chassis. In 1967 chassis builders like Woody Gilmore, George Britting, and the Logghe brothers were working overtime to satisfy the racers who wanted to race Funny Cars.

In 1967 the Logghe brothers built the *Eliminator II* for Don Nicholson. This car looked identical to the first, except for the roof hatch above the driver. Nicholson's competition was closing in, and at the end of 1967 he added a supercharger to his *Eliminator II*. "It was tough to beat the blown cars," says Nicholson. "Late in 1967 Pete Robinson loaned me a blown motor from his dragster."

Nicholson's first outing with the blown Cammer was at a match race in Delaware. The first run with the new engine produced an easy win. "In the second round, my car started to climb up in the air—we didn't have any wheelie bars at the time. It kept climbing, and I shut it off when I couldn't see where I was going. When I got ready to run the third round, the strip operator came over and yelled, 'That's enough!' He was scared to death."

Funny Cars continued to be a drag-racing promoter's dream. In 1967, Orange County International Raceway in Southern California held a Manufacturers' Championship. In the late 1960s, the Chrysler Hemi was not the predominate engine in the Funny Car class. Ford Cammers, Big-Block Chevys, and even a few Pontiac engines were also powering Funny Cars. This diverse mix of engines and corporate bodies allowed the promoters to play on the natural automotive biases of the race fans. Ford vs. Chevy or Chrysler vs. Pontiac match races would have the crowd cheering as if it were the Christians versus the lions. Track announcers did their best at these events to whip the crowd into a frenzy.

In 1967 everyone was getting into the act. The Ramchargers team from Detroit built a 1967 Dodge Dart Funny Car. Like its contemporaries, the Dart featured a tube chassis, but instead of an all-fiberglass body, the Ramchargers Dart had an acid-dipped steel body with a fiberglass lift-off roof. It was unique because its entire roof could be removed. Mickey Thompson was working on a Pontiac Firebird with a blown Chrysler Hemi, and Doug "Cookie" Cook of the Stone Woods and Cook Gasser fame was running a supercharged Mustang Funny Car. Veteran racer Hayden Proffitt even ran a 1967 Rambler Funny Car powered by a bored and stroked American Motors 343-ci engine. The Funny Cars had something for everybody.

By the end of the decade, every major Funny Car competitor was running a supercharged engine in a tube chassis with a flip-top body. Elapsed times were in the mid-seven second range at speeds in excess of 190 miles per hour.

Rich Guasco was involved in all phases of hot rodding. In addition to winning the America's Most Beautiful Roadster award at the 1961 Oakland Roadster Show, he raced dragsters and Fuel Altereds. In the early 1970s, he built this Dodge Demon Funny Car. Like his Fuel Altered, the Funny Car was flamed and named Pure Hell. With Dave Bebee driving, this car won the 1973 NHRA Springnationals. Ron Lewis

FUNNY CAR FEVER

In the mid-1960s, Top Fuel dragsters were the main attraction at the strip. At the 1965 Bakersfield Fuel and Gas Championship, also known as the March Meet, there were 64 of the nation's top nitro-burning dragsters in the staging lanes. The 1966 March Meet also fielded 64 dragsters. But the following year some of the biggest names in Top Fuel dragsters passed up the event, leaving only 32 entries. The March Meet of 1967 was promoted as a Funny Car event. Funny Cars were becoming as popular as Top Fuel dragsters and that popularity was growing. The Funny Car had become an integral part of the drag-racing landscape nationwide, and this new class of racing became a permanent fixture at national events. The winner of the first Funny Car championship at the 1967 NHRA Nationals was Doug Thorley driving Doug's Headers Corvair.

Although the Funny Car was popular with fans, many veteran Top Fuel drivers had a different opinion of this upstart rival—at least initially. Ed McCulloch, who would eventually go on to become one of the top drivers in the 1980s and a noted crew chief in the 1990s, owned and ran his own Top Fuel dragster in 1969. He was a good friend of Art Whipple, who had purchased a 1969 Camaro Funny Car. Whipple asked McCulloch to help him with the car at his first race at Balboa Park, in Eugene, Oregon. McCulloch recalls the experience. "I was a dragster guy and didn't want to hear anything about Funny Cars. Funny Cars were junk! But I drove the car to check it out and ended up qualifying Number One." Needless to say, Art Whipple never got to drive the car. McCulloch continued to run the car for Whipple throughout the 1969 season. The car ran well, could always qualify easily, and would generally beat the competition on the first run. But the Chevy engine was unreliable. McCulloch would joke that it was always better to race against him in the second round, when his Chevy engine was almost certain to blow up.

Mr. Norm's Grand Spaulding Dodge started sponsoring race cars in the early 1960s to increase floor traffic at the dealership. Mr. Norm's moved into the Funny Car ranks when they became more popular than Super Stocks. This unrestored Dodge Charger Funny Car was found a few years ago, minus the engine, in the back of a body shop in Chicago.

Ed McCulloch had a hard time adjusting to a Funny Car after driving Top Fuel dragsters. The old Funny Cars had a wide frame with a small bucket seat, an automatic transmission, and a little round steering wheel. As a driver, McCulloch felt horribly confined as the body was put down into place. As he continued to race the Funny Car, the feeling of confinement soon changed to one of security, even though the only protection between him and the engine consisted of a ridiculously thin piece of aluminum. From then on, when the body came down, he was ready to race.

By the end of 1968, McCulloch sold his Top Fuel dragster and Art Whipple sold his Camaro Funny Car. They put everything they had into a professionally built Funny Car. This was at a time when Top Fuel racing wasn't the money-making venture it is today. Many drivers were switching to Funny Cars, because that was where the money was.

For the 1970 season, McCulloch and Whipple campaigned a Duster, a state-of-the-art vehicle built by Dick Fletcher. It was one of the first cars with a narrow chassis and a dragster-style roll cage. They also spent money on a more powerful and reliable engine—a Chrysler Hemi built by Keith Black. The Duster had full side windows and a roof hatch, and all of the aluminum was anodized. Before the car was even finished, they took it to the 1970 Winternationals. The car qualified with a top speed of 204.

Ed McCulloch would go on to become one of the sport's best Funny Car drivers. He won 18 national events in a Funny Car and then switched back to Top Fuel in 1992.

There, he would win four more national events. He admits to one auspicious Funny Car loss. "John Force beat me for his first national event win," confides McCulloch. "Up until that time, we used to whip him like a stepchild!" Since retiring from behind the wheel, McCulloch has become one of the nation's best Top Fuel and Funny Car crew chiefs.

In the early 1960s in Kenosha, Wisconsin, John Buttera and his friend Dennis Rollain teamed up and opened R&B Automotive. They earned a good reputation for building and repairing race cars. That reputation extended down to Chicago, where Gary Dyer

Roof hatches were not mandatory for Funny Cars when this car was built in the late 1960s. Drivers entered and exited through one of the open side windows or when the body was open. The white stripe across the nose was added when the body developed a large transverse crack. The metal flake color of the car was not paint, but a feature of the fiberglass gelcoat. The only way to cover the repair was by adding a stripe.

Mr. Norm's Super Charger *was one of the many Funny Cars with a sleek Dodge Charger body. The front wheels were moved forward, while the rest of the body retained much of the original shape and proportion. Gary Dyer drove this car for Mr. Norm. Jere Alhadeff*

was racing for Norm "Mr. Norm" Kraus. He contracted with R&B for a new Funny Car. "We built this car, and it was horrible—but it was OK for back then. It would be an embarrassment if anybody rolled it out today," recalled the ever-modest Buttera. "Dyer had a blown Chrysler in it. He won the races he should have won, and he lost the races he should have lost." Buttera's skills were noticed

by others and he was soon asked to build other chassis.

Not everyone was lucky enough to have factory backing or the ability to pull a mold for a fiberglass Funny Car body off of a styling model, as was done for Nicholson's *Eliminator I.* Most early Funny Car bodies were made by local suppliers. To create the mold for a full-size car body, these inventive rascals would drop by their local car rental agency and rent a car with the body desired by the racer.

"That's mainly where the molds came from for those cars," recalls Buttera with a laugh. "They would clay up the door jams of the rental car and pull a mold off the thing. They usually wound up pulling off most of the paint and killing all the chrome. Then they would try and get it back together, park it in a bad part of town, and report it stolen! Everything was an adventure back then."

Buttera's talent was recognized by Mickey Thompson at the 1968 U.S. Nationals. Thompson had a shop on the West Coast, where he was building several cars. Thompson offered Buttera a job and he accepted. When he arrived at Thompson's shop, he was amazed at the craftsmen Thompson had working for him. "There were all these icons—people you couldn't even believe you were standing next to. And me—I'm a complete rube." Buttera is as much a craftsman as he is self-effacing. He blended in

The parachutes have just blossomed on the L.A. Hooker in the near lane. The L.A. Hooker was owned by Gene Beaver, John Force's cousin and drag-racing mentor. In the 1960s and 1970s, Funny Car drivers and cars had catchy nicknames. Unfortunately for Beaver, many track owners found the name of his car offensive and refused to book him for match races. Ron Lewis

Climbing out from under the Ford EXP body is the Blue Max owner/driver, Raymond Beadle. Beadle was one of the superstars of Funny Car racing. Booking his Blue Max would guarantee the promoter a sellout for a match race. In addition to match racing, Beadle won three consecutive NHRA Funny Car Championships from 1979 through 1981. Ron Lewis

well and continued to refine his car-building craft. He also enjoyed the access to the aviation industry and its surplus parts. Back home in Wisconsin, Buttera would go to Sears and Roebuck, Montgomery Wards, or the corner auto parts store for parts. In California, he was like a kid in a candy store because of the extensive supply of surplus aircraft components. "On Saturdays, instead of going to Disneyland, I spent hours just looking through boxes and shelves of surplus stuff. I'd see a bracket or something that would just spark my imagination by the way it was built or designed."

Buttera continued to develop his skills by working with two legends of the sport—engine builder Keith Black and chassis builder Woody Gilmore. "I learned a lot from working at Black's and I learned *so* much from working at Woody's," exclaimed Buttera. One of the biggest heartbreaks of Buttera's life was the day Woody had to let him go.

Buttera had been assembling a small collection of tools and rented a 1,400-square-foot shop in Cerritos, California. He made a living by plumbing fuel and brake lines for race cars. One morning he received a call from Don Schumacher asking him to build a

Funny Car. Buttera explained that he couldn't build Schumacher a car because he didn't have enough equipment. Jim Annin, one of the friends Buttera made while working at Keith Black's shop, agreed to loan Buttera $5,000 to get his shop set up. Annin told Buttera, "I'll lend you the $5,000, and when you get good at Funny Cars—I've got one comin'." Buttera replied, "Cool."

He stocked his shop with the tools he needed and started on Schumacher's car. He used a chassis design similar to one on a Funny Car he had built at Mickey Thompson's. It had an independent front end and a sprung rear end. The engine was a blown Chrysler built by Ed Pink. At that time, August 1970, no one in California had made a six-second run in a Funny Car, and Orange Country International Raceway (OCIR), in Irvine, California, had put up $5,000 for the first Funny Car to do it. Buttera and Schumacher took the new car out to OCIR to shake it down. It was a Saturday night, and all the big names in Funny Cars were there. Everybody was trying to run in the sixes. After a half pass to make sure the new car was mechanically sound, Schumacher climbed back in for a full pass.

Raymond Beadle's gawky-looking Ford EXP enters the timing lights at speed. In 1982, when this photo was taken, Funny Car aerodynamic development was in its infancy. Within a few years, wind tunnel testing would become an important component of Funny Car body development. Ron Lewis

In the early 1970s, Don "The Snake" Prudhomme switched from dragsters to Funny Cars. His friend and fellow drag racer Tom "The Mongoose" McEwen brought him in on a deal with Mattel Toy Company to promote Hot Wheels toy cars. Prudhomme, like many other dragster drivers, initially disliked Funny Cars, but soon fell in love with the way they drove and with the financial opportunities they offered.

"Schumacher takes it up to the starting line and makes a 6.93 pass," says Buttera. "The whole grandstand fell apart—everybody was screaming and jumping up and down. After that one pass, we put the car on the trailer, took the $5,000 and headed for Indy—won the Nationals, and like they say, the rest is history." By the time Buttera got back from Indianapolis, his phone was ringing off the hook. In the early 1970s, every big name Funny Car racer in the country wanted a Buttera-built Funny Car.

Don Schumacher was a charter member in the Funny Car racing fraternity. Driving a Funny Car, he won 5 NHRA events, 9 IHRA events, and 13 AHRA events, and he was the AHRA National Champion in 1973 and the IHRA National Champion in 1972.

Funny Car shows drew the biggest crowds at the drag strip. Bill Doner and Steve Evans were the fathers of the big Funny Car shows on the West Coast. Evans, along with Doner, managed all the top tracks on the West Coast,

John Buttera built this car for Prudhomme in 1973, when it was sponsored by Carefree Gum. Buttera's chassis were finely crafted assemblies that were rigid, lightweight, and drove well. Funny Car engines were simpler then, with only one small fuel pump and a single magneto.

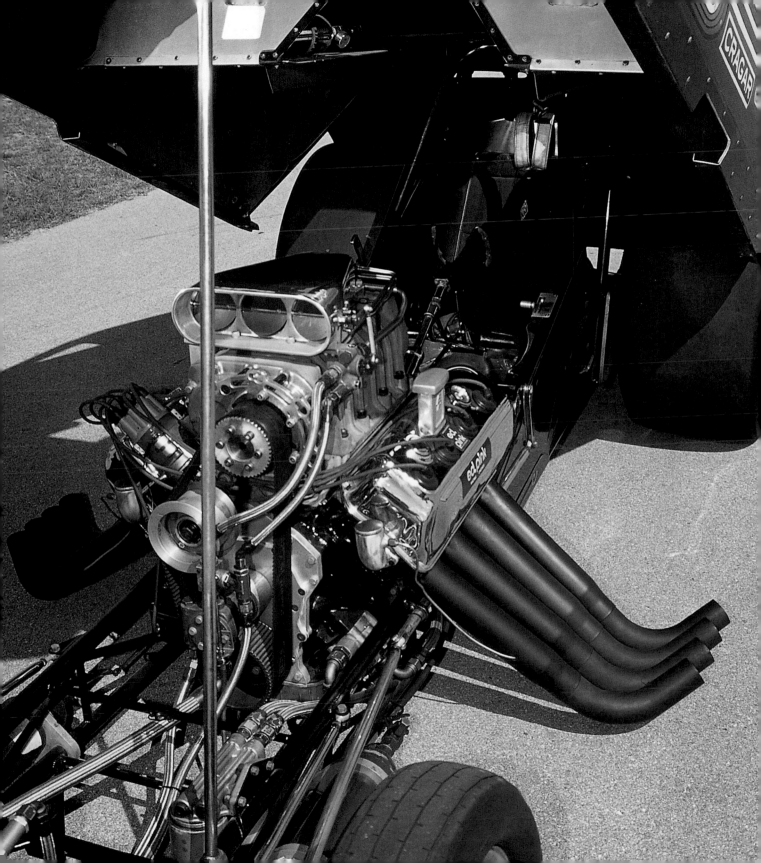

In 1973, Prudhomme had the U.S. Army as a sponsor for his Funny Car. Part of the agreement included visits to schools with recruiters. At the track, an Army recruiter would be in the pits handing out posters and information. "They told me years later," recalls Prudhomme, "that it was one of the best recruiting tools the Army ever had."

In the early 1980s, John Force followed the nickname trend set by so many other drivers when he became "Brute" Force. Here, in his Mountain Dew-sponsored Funny Car, he has a small lead on Raymond Beadle. Ron Lewis

Racing a Funny Car can be a dangerous business, as the driver of the Mountain Monza *learned when it blew up while entering the lights. The entire underside of the car is engulfed and even a few flames are licking up into the driver's compartment. The driver had just reached up with his right hand to release the drag chute. Ron Lewis*

including OCIR. Orange County had been famous for Funny Car competition under its original management; it used to have a race called the Manufacturer's Championship. At that time it was possible to stock a field with cars powered by different brands of motors. But soon all the cars were running the Hemi engine. "I remember the first time I ran 32 Funny Cars at Irwindale," exclaims Evans. "Oh, God, did we jam that place!" Soon, Funny Car shows were drawing as many as 64 cars. Along with the cars came the characters and roustabouts associated with the formative days of Funny Car racing.

"We had tons and tons of touring cars from all over the country," says Evans. "That's what they did for a living. The *Chi-Town Hustler* was a big draw, and of course, so were Prudhomme, and McEwen. The *Blue Max* was just a killer car in Southern California. We spent a lot of money booking those cars; some were as cheap as $750 and others as much as $3,500. But "Jungle Jim" Lieberman was Number One—he ran the most dates in a year."

Getting warm bodies in the seats when Jungle Jim was running was as easy as giving away free beer at a July baseball game. He was a one-man unpredictable extravaganza.

Ed "The Ace" McCulloch was one of the top Funny Car drivers. In 1973 he started a long relationship with the Revell company that produced models of the Funny Car he drove. This car has an interesting wing arrangement in front of the rear tire. McCulloch won 18 national events while driving a Funny Car and 4 behind the wheel of a Top Fuel dragster. Jere Alhadeff

"Jungle Jim was always doing stuff," says Evans. "One day we had all the Funny Cars lined up in two rows and Jungle did a burnout right down the middle of 'em. I got a letter from NHRA on that." Jungle Jim was the king of match races. He would run as many as three cars, and he constantly irritated the track operators. He would double book and only make one event, or send one of his cars with another driver. "You had to have him," explains Evans. "You had to have Jungle if you were going to run a Funny Car race on the West Coast. If you didn't have him, he was conspicuous by his absence."

One night in Portland, Oregon, Jungle was to run Gordy Bonin in the final. The show was running late and Jungle came out for the final, but Bonin had blown his engine. Jungle made a single. On the burnout, he intentionally knocked over the plastic barrel that holds the water. He came back and did another burnout. He staged, found some dry pavement on the right-hand side, and set the track record. The next thing the crowd saw was Jungle coming down the return road in the back of a pickup truck. He was playing a guitar and harmonica while singing, "Michael Row Your Boat Ashore." He followed that act up by doing bird calls in the Winner's Circle.

"Jungle Jim was the best showman of 'em all," says John Force. Jungle Jim never won a national event or a championship, but the fans loved him. "The first time I ever saw Jungle Jim race was at Irwindale Raceway," says Force. "I watched this guy do burnouts to the lights, turn around, drive back down the return road. I thought, what is he doing?" Force had the pleasure of being a bit player in one of Jungle's shows one Saturday night at OCIR. "I had to race Jungle in the final and I never

OCIR in Irvine, California, had some of the biggest Funny Car meets. With as many as 64 cars, promoters ran a "Chicago Style" show, in which the field would be paired off and the two fastest drivers would meet at the end of the night to determine the overall winner. Here, Ed McCulloch (near lane) is lined up against "Big Jim" Dunn in his rear-engined Funny Car. Ed McCulloch collection

In 1967, Austin Coil joined up with John Farkonas and Pat Minick to form the Chi-Town Hustler team. Coil's tuning ability led the team to National Championships in 1982 and 1983. In 1985, Coil joined John Force and within a few years, Force became National Champion. Ron Lewis

beat anybody in those days." Because of a problem with his car, Jungle couldn't make it in time for the start of the race and the promoter required Force to race a single. "I did my burnout and as I was backing up to stage, here comes Jungle!" Because Liberman didn't make the start time, the track officials wouldn't let him onto the track to run. Undaunted, Liberman did a burnout down the return road. "I was looking over trying to figure out what he was doing," says Force. "You can't do that, I thought to myself."

Force made his single run, but his car broke and stopped on the track short of the finish line. The crowd was gathering at the far end of the track yelling and cheering, as Force was out of his car pushing it the remaining way. "When I shoved my car across the line, the win light came on," says Force. "This was a big deal to me—I pushed my car across to beat Jungle Jim. The next thing I know, Jungle Jim's car is comin' down the return road again. The roof hatch opens, he jumps out of the car and comes over and starts beating up this guy on the back of the fire truck. It was a big old fight and I was in shock." That day, Force had sold one of his old fire suits to one of the track safety crew—the guy who took the beating. Wearing a helmet, he looked like John Force from a distance, and ended up as the recipient of Jungle's onslaught.

44

"Jungle Jim" Liberman was the king of match races. He never won a National event, but Jungle Jim drew the biggest crowds wherever he appeared. His first Funny Car was the Brutus GTO, followed by a series of Chevys, like this early Nova. Ron Lewis

"When we got back to the pits, Beaver (Gene Beaver was John Force's cousin, and Force called him 'Uncle Beaves' most of the time) said, 'Jungle is mad; I know him, let's go over and fix it.' Beaver took Force over to Jungle's car in the pits. Force was scared to death. Beaver said to Jungle, "I want you to meet my cousin, Johnny."

"I was intimidated," recalls Force. "I was 21 years old, and here's a guy that's a god, that you read about in magazines. Jungle looked over at me and said, 'Oh, hi, John.' I was waiting for him to slug me." Beaver asked Jungle if he was still mad at Force. Jungle looked at Force and said, "Why would I be mad at you?" Force went on to explain to Jungle that the track officials told him he wouldn't be paid if he didn't run. And the guy Jungle beat up at the end of the track really wasn't him, but a track worker. "I think the drugs dropped down to a level," says Force. "And then Jungle said to me, 'Oh, was that your car I raced in the final? It was all part of the show.' "John Force was amazed. "Jungle Jim didn't know who I was," says Force, "and the fans were all around his car—I won the race and nobody was around my car." Within a few years that would change.

John Force learned a lot from his fellow drivers. From Jungle Jim Liberman he learned showmanship. Jungle Jim was the

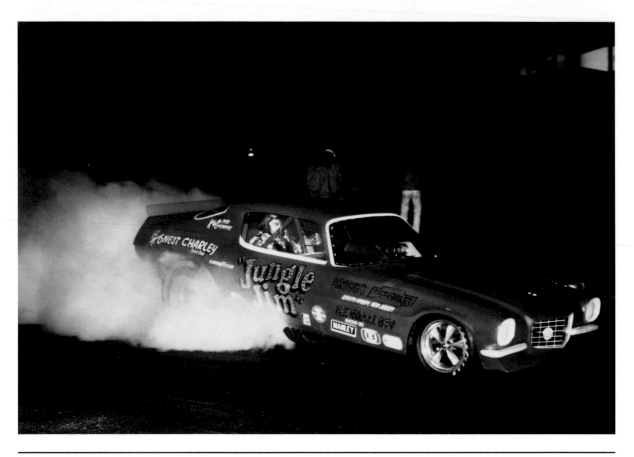

Jungle Jim's unpredictability was one of the keys to his success. Long burnouts were standard fare for Liberman. He understood the importance of showmanship and the fans always got their money's worth when he raced, even if he didn't win. Jere Alhadeff

right guy at the right time in the Funny Car world, but his career was cut short by a fatal automobile accident on September 9, 1977. If he were alive today, he wouldn't be able to survive in the corporate-bound race environment. Force learned that side of the game elsewhere. "I always joke that three people taught me the business," says Force. "Don Prudhomme taught me how to be motivated and race, Tom "The Mongoose" McEwen taught me how to hustle money from corporate America, but I learned the most from Raymond Beadle. He taught me how to wheel and deal."

Raymond Beadle's *Blue Max* was one of the most popular Funny Cars on the circuit. "The car was beautiful with the big gold German cross on it," says Steve Evans. "Beadle just had charisma. He was probably the sexiest Funny Car driver ever and the gals loved him." Along with being a match race favorite, Beadle also won three NHRA championships (1979, 1980, and 1981). Racer Gene Snow once quipped about Beadle, "I don't know how anybody who walks so slow and talks that slow can think that fast." It was said that Beadle didn't walk—he moseyed. Raymond Beadle invented the apparel business in drag racing with his halter tops for the girls. One of Beadle's most memorable moments was when he rolled his car during a race in Gainesville, Florida. The car, minus the body, landed upright and Beadle quickly exited and casually waved to the crowd. After proving himself as a winner in drag racing, Beadle moved on to NASCAR. He teamed up with driver Rusty Wallace and promptly won the championship. "I think Beadle's transition to NASCAR, where he picked the right driver and right crew chief and won the NASCAR championship, was awesome," says Force.

John Force's accomplishments can also be called awesome. The decade of the 1990s can be summed up in one five-letter word—FORCE. Force devastated the Funny Car competition like a spring tornado cutting through a Kansas trailer park. He won an unprece-dent-ed nine Funny Car titles and collected 76 national event wins. During the period from 1990 to 1999, Funny Car elapsed times

Don Schumacher was one of the top Funny Car racers in the early 1970s. He won more than 20 national events. He was the IHRA National Champion in 1972 and the AHRA National Champion in 1973. Schumacher proved that there were hazards to doing long burnouts. Filling the driver's compartment of his Barracuda with tire smoke was one of them. Jere Alhadeff

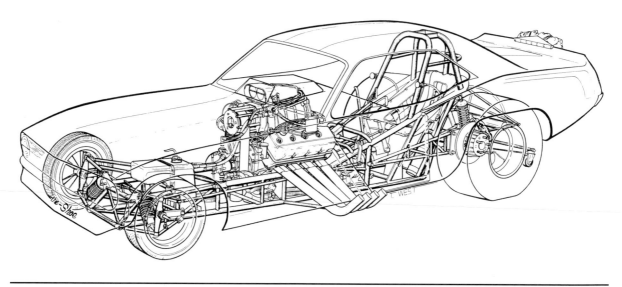

By the early 1970s, Funny Car chassis design was as advanced as that of any other high-tech race car. Front suspension designs, like the one on Schumacher's Barracuda, were the result of years of development and taking some of the best innovations from the Indy car world. With improvements in tire technology came lower elapsed times and higher speeds. Tom West

dropped from 5.13 to 4.77 seconds and speeds rose from 283.28 to 324.05 miles per hour. While finishing up the decade with both ends of the Funny Car national record, Force didn't always lead the way in lower elapsed times and spectacular speeds. What he did was establish a team that gave him a mechanical combination that was reliable. Then he supported his team by being the best behind the wheel.

Force was not born with a silver spoon in his mouth or a wealth of knowledge about race cars. "The first race I saw was at Lions Drag Strip," recalls Force. "That was just before Funny Cars, in 1964 or 1965. The first car I took to the drag strip was a 1960 Ford Fairlane with a 428 Interceptor motor with a broken motor mount. I remember how scared I was; I didn't know what the Christmas tree was." Force was fascinated by drag-racing professionals such as Prudhomme and Garlits. "I just

wanted to feel what it was like to race a car like the big guys—they were just gods." Force's first real race car was an Olds-powered dragster that blew up on his first pass down the strip. Steve Evans recalls, "I may have signed John Force's first NHRA license. I remember saying, 'Dead Man Walking.' For Force to have survived his early years is unbelievable. The Funny Cars of the late 1960s early 1970s were dangerous—really, really dangerous."

Force struggled for many years before getting a break. His cousin, Gene Beaver, had been racing in Australia, and he invited John to come down and race. When Force came back to the States, he was able to get a better car, and he started to tour.

One of the smartest things Force ever did was hire Austin Coil as his crew chief. Coil had tuned the *Chi-Town Hustler* to two National Championships (1982 and 1983). With a lack of funding, the team was folding

In the mid-1980s, Funny Cars became more streamlined and looked less like a standard passenger car. Ed McCulloch's wedge-shaped Miller Oldsmobile was developed in the wind tunnel. Also at that time, engine technology was taking some giant leaps with the use of aluminum heads and advanced fuel systems. *Ron Lewis*

up its tent. Force's cousin, Beaver, is the one who encouraged him to hire Coil. Beaver told Force, "He's about to quit because they're out of money. With your B.S. and his talent, you guys could be champions." Beaver encouraged Force to talk to Coil and tell him he had a $100,000 budget to race on. Force told Coil he would give him $10,000 to join his team. Force didn't have the money and had to go to three people to borrow it.

Force and Coil agreed to meet in Phoenix. "We were in a Mexican restaurant," recalls Force. "I remember going in there, because I was shaking." At that meeting he told Coil that he wanted him to run his car and that he had plenty of money.

Three years later they were fighting it out. Force recalls, "I told Coil, 'You told me I was going to win the championship!' And he said, 'Yeah, and you said you had a million dollars—so we both lied.'" Since then, Force and Coil have become the best of friends. Coil is the brains behind setting up the Castrol Funny Car, and Force never questions him.

"He's the most honest man I've ever met," says Force with a big grin. "In the beginning, the money I paid him was more than my sponsorship. Part of the reason I got Castrol as a sponsor was because they asked if Austin Coil was going to stay with me. I said yeah, and they gave me a $5,000 decal for the front of my car. That's how it started."

Each Funny Car race team has a shop where the team assembles its cars and stores the spare parts needed to race. In the off-season, this is the team's home. This is Don Prudhomme's Snake Racing shop floor in Vista, California. In addition to the U.S. Tobucco Funny Car, he also runs the Miller Lite Top Fuel dragster. The shop floor is littered with engines and Funny Car and Top Fuel chassis in various stages of completion.

ANATOMY OF A FUNNY CAR

The NHRA Media Guide defines the Funny Car as follows: "Funny Cars are short-wheelbase cars with a composite replica of a production car body. The engines are identical to those that power Top Fuel machines, with one noticeable difference—they are located in front of the driver. The minimum weight of a Funny Car, including the driver, is 2,325 pounds." What the media guide fails to tell the reader in its basic statement is that Funny Cars produce the best drag-racing show on earth!

Today's Funny Cars are as sophisticated as any modern NASCAR (National Association for Stock Car Auto Racing), CART (Championship Auto Racing Teams), or IRL (Indy Racing League) race car. They are designed with incredible speed and safety in mind. Amazingly, the NHRA's rules for a fuel Funny Car are rather simple and straightforward, covering only six pages in its rule book. Several other pages are devoted to safety concerns, such as roll cage construction, clutch shields, and driver protective clothing. These safety issues also apply to classes other than Funny Cars.

The engine in today's Funny Car must be of a V-8 automotive design with a displacement of between 490 and 500 ci. There is no transmission—only a reverser. The rear end is limited to a 3.20 ratio and the rear slicks are limited to 18 inches wide with a 118-inch circumference. The wheelbase is restricted to between 100 and 125 inches. The body must be modeled after a 1995 or later mass-produced automobile, domestic or foreign. One look at a Funny Car and it's apparent that body modifications are allowed, including a 2-inch top chop. Spoilers and wings are also allowed. To keep the playing field as level as possible, NHRA imposes several restrictions on body modifications.

The Engine

Funny Cars cannot run any type of engine. The rules dictate an internal combustion, reciprocating, 90-degree V-8 automotive type engine. It must have a single camshaft, ruling out multi-camshaft overhead cam engines. And only two valves per cylinder are allowed. The minimum displacement for a Funny Car engine is 490 ci and the maximum is 500. There are two bore and stroke combinations used: 4.18 bore x 4.50 stroke (called a 3/4 stroker) and 4.25 bore x 4.38 stroke (called a 5/8 stroker). The 4.18 x 4.50 combination, equaling 496 ci, is the most common in the Funny Car ranks.

The Chrysler Hemi has always been a favorite of racers, but a production version would not be practical where such high combustion pressures are attained. The rules allow the use of aftermarket engines that are similar

An NHRA Funny Car's engine is limited to a V-8 automotive design with a maximum of 500 ci. It must run a single camshaft and have a maximum of two valves per cylinder. All Funny Car engines are based on the Chrysler Hemi design. Roots-type superchargers are allowed and everybody runs one. The inlet on the injector is limited to 65 square inches. This engine is about to be test fired in the pits. Attached to the supercharger's snout is an electric starter. An auxiliary fuel pressure gauge is alongside the supercharger.

Funny Car engines use aluminum connecting rods. Because of the high loads induced into these rods, they are constantly checked to see if they have either lengthened or shortened in length. Components like these rods are bought by the case.

diameter, made of titanium, and exhaust valves are 1.90-inch diameter, made of Inconel. The valves must be actuated by the engine's single camshaft. The single camshaft is a long-duration type with roller lifters. A dry sump oiling system is allowed and virtually every competitor runs one.

The engine's supercharger is limited to a Roots type, similar to the GM 71-series. Maximum size is 14-71 with a 19-inch rotor case length and 11.25-inch width. A variable speed drive system for the blower is not allowed. Funny Car superchargers are belt-driven off of the crankshaft pulley. Pulleys of a larger or smaller diameter can be swapped, altering the supercharger's output. This modification is called changing the overdrive. Each Funny Car must have a restraint system that will contain a supercharger explosion. A special blanket of ballistic material wraps the supercharger for this purpose. The supercharger manifold must also have a burst panel that will open

in design to an automotive engine. All current Funny Cars use an aluminum block. Until recently, all Top Fuel and Funny Car blocks have been made of cast aluminum. The latest technology in this area has produced a forged aluminum block. These blocks, while slightly heavier, are much stronger. No matter the manufacturer, an aluminum block must have sleeves fitted to the cylinders. These sleeves are made from centrifugally cast ductile iron, precisely machined, and pressed into the block. Aluminum pistons and connecting rods are used. The crankshaft is made from billet chrome-vanadium steel, which weighs in at 79 pounds. The Hemi-style cylinder heads are manufactured from billet aluminum. The intake valves are 2.40-inch

In the late 1990s, the forged aluminum cylinder block was introduced. It's a little heavier than the cast blocks, but it's also much stronger. This block has the cylinder head studs in place. The piston in the foreground (Number 7) is at top dead center. The top surface of the piston and part of the cylinder sleeve are notched for intake valve clearance.

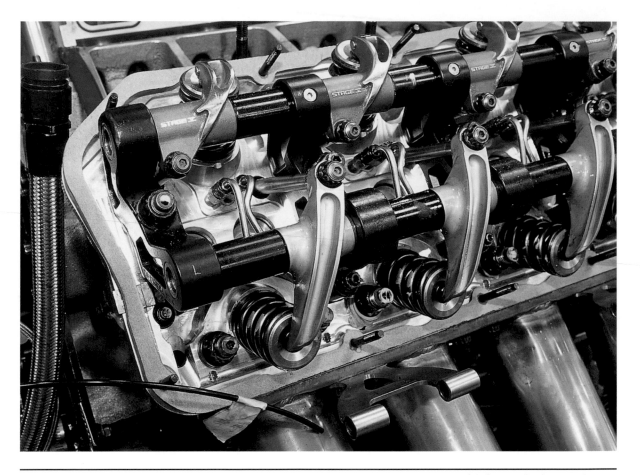

The Hemi cylinder heads used on all Funny Cars are made from billet aluminum. Under the valve cover are two sets of shaft-mounted rocker arms. The upper set is for the intake valves and the lower set is for the exhaust valves. Plumbed into each intake port, just behind the intake valve, is a pair of fuel lines.

in case of a backfire, preventing a catastrophic supercharger explosion. Sitting on top of the supercharger is the fuel injector. Its air inlet opening is limited to 65 square inches. Electronic, pneumatic, or hydraulic throttles are not allowed. The control of the fuel injector's butterflies is manually actuated by the driver's foot. One thing that is allowed is a throttle stop that restricts the injector opening during burnouts.

Carbon fiber composite construction is allowed on the fuel injector, but not on the oil pan or valve covers. The exhaust headers must be double-pipe insulated construction from the flange on the cylinder head down to where the bend is made at the bottom edge of the body.

The fuel system is the heart of the Funny Car engine. The crankshaft-driven fuel pump will deliver from 500 to 600 pounds of fuel pressure at as much as 75 gallons per minute. During a single quarter-mile run, a Funny Car will burn 5 gallons of fuel. A single run—including starting, the burnout, backing up, staging, and the quarter-mile run—will consume as much as 15

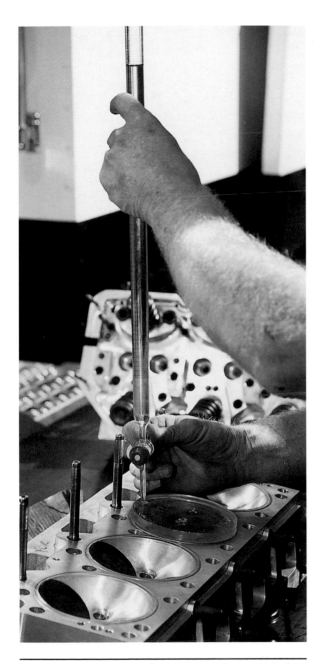

Cylinder heads are checked with a burette to make sure each of the combustion chambers contains the same volume (approximately 170 cc). This operation, where the volume is checked in cubic centimeters, is known as "cc-ing." The combustion chamber volume is a critical component in determining the engine's compression ratio.

Mounted on the front of the engine is the fuel pump, which is driven off the camshaft. One of the reasons nitro-burning Funny Cars run so fast is the amount of fuel this pump delivers. In one minute, this pump is able to deliver 75 gallons of fuel at pressures of 500 to 600 psi. The small red frame on the front of the intake manifold holds the burst panel. It is designed to prevent a catastrophic explosion by opening, should a backfire occur.

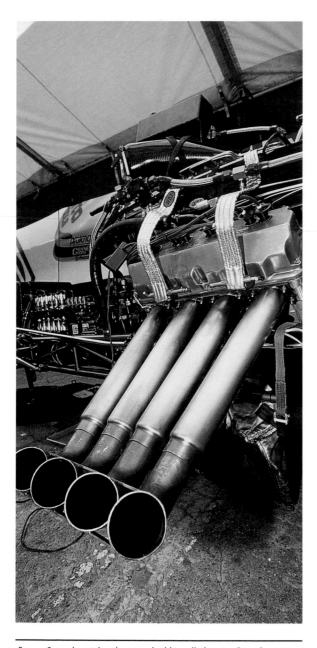

Funny Car exhaust headers are double-walled to insulate the portion that is inside the body. Attached to each pipe is a temperature sensor that is connected to the data recording computer. The two straps that wrap over the valve covers are part of the restraint system designed to keep parts from becoming projectiles in the event of a catastrophic explosion.

gallons. A fuel Funny Car runs on a mix of nitromethane and alcohol. Nitromethane (which is produced by nitrating propane) costs approximately $30 per gallon. The average passenger car runs on a 12-to-1 mixture of air and gasoline. A fuel Funny Car will run air-fuel mixtures as high as one-to-one. Nitromethane provides tremendous amounts of horsepower. A nitromethane-burning fuel Funny Car is 66 miles per hour faster and .81 seconds quicker than a Federal Mogul Funny Car, which runs only on alcohol. Prior to the year 2000, fuel Funny Cars were allowed to run any percentage of nitro desired. Mixtures of 98 to 99 percent nitromethane and 2 or 1 percent alcohol were common. For the 2000 season, NHRA has limited the maximum amount of nitro to 90 percent.

Several sets of nozzles provide fuel to the engine. There are six or eight in the injector. These are to provide a small amount of lubrication to the blower's impellers. The majority of the fuel nozzles are in the intake manifold and cylinder heads. These nozzles provide most of the fuel needed to produce upward of 6,000 horsepower. The nozzles in the intake, one or two at each port, are spaced around each of the intake ports. Within each intake port on the cylinder head are two nozzles just upstream from the intake valve. These nozzles are the last to be fed fuel during the run. They typically have an in-line pressure check valve to limit fuel flow to certain levels of fuel pressure. Fuel delivery is controlled by a series of pneumatically controlled timers. These timers vary the fuel mixture and are set incrementally for different time periods during the run.

While not rated at a certain compression ratio, Funny Car engines run compression ratios between 6:1 and 7:1. Crew

The crew of this Funny Car is in the last stages of preparation prior to test firing in the pits. The two red units to the left are the twin magnetos. There are two plugs per cylinder on a Funny Car, and each magneto fires a plug at the same time in each cylinder. The crewman on the right has his hand on the injector hat. Just below his hand is the barrel valve through which flows all the fuel for the engine.

chiefs, when talking about engine compression ratio, have a baseline and then refer to compression ratio changes by the difference in piston height. They may say that a "piston is 10 down." That means that a certain piston is .010 lower than its baseline piston; "40 down" would be a piston .040 lower than baseline. One interesting point about supercharged nitro engines is that not all of the cylinders run the same compression ratio. The compression ratio between cylinders from front to back increases slightly in each cylinder. This is because the helical design of the blower impellers causes more fuel to end up in the manifold for the rear cylinders of the engine. The front cylinders get a higher percentage of the blower's air and less fuel. Typically the

FUNNY CAR PRICES AREN'T FUNNY

So you think you'd like to go Funny Car racing? Before you pull on your helmet, take a deep breath and look at some of the basic costs involved.

Chassis	$34,000
Composite body	15,000
Billet rear end	18,000
Goodyear 18x36-inch slicks (per pair)	900
Parachutes (two required) (each)	1,000
On-board data recorder	20,000
Four-disc clutch	8,350
Reverser	2,500
Fire suppression system	1,500
Engine block	5,000
Heads, per pair, bare	5,400
Cam and valvetrain	6,000
Pistons, per set	400
Rods, per set	720
Fuel pump	2,500
Injector with pump & barrel valve	7,000
Double magneto	11,000
Nitro, per gallon (15 gallons per run)	30

With all the extras, the cost of a single, complete ready-to-race Funny Car is approximately $200,000. Most teams have two complete cars and lots of spares. To transport that car, you'll need a diesel tractor with a custom-built trailer. A good used unit can be found for between $200,000 and $300,000. Then you'll need to hire a top-notch crew chief and crew to make it all work. The total cost to run a professional Funny Car for one year is more than $1 million.

farther forward the cylinder, the leaner it runs. Therefore, the fuel nozzles are richer in the front of the engine than those in the rear. The overall compression ratio is controlled by the thickness of the head gasket used. The crew chief maintains a large selection of gaskets with various thicknesses. These gaskets are made of copper.

When looking at a Funny Car engine, it's easy to see that there are two spark plugs per cylinder and two magnetos—two complete ignition systems. The two magnetos are connected by a cog belt. Each of these systems fires at exactly the same time in each cylinder. Timing is one of the critical tuning components, and crew chiefs will set the ignition to within one-half of one degree accuracy. There is also a device that retards the timing at a certain point in the run. At approximately one second into the run, the timing is retarded slightly for approximately one second or less. This is a critical point in the run where too much horsepower can hurt, more than help. There are two ways to retard the ignition, with an air-activated solenoid or with a retard chip in the ignition module.

Tuning one of these engines is more difficult than one might think. "We will vary compression ratios, blower ratios, fuel volume, ignition timing, and nitro percentage," says Bernie Fedderly, John Force's crew chief. "These are the key tuning components. We will look at ambient weather conditions and plug in the factors. These engines are tricky—the sun goes behind a cloud and you've got a different animal. A five degree temperature drop is a big influence. We work in tenths of a percent of nitro, half-degrees of timing, and a few thousandths of compression—these things are a little more sensitive than one would think."

A minimum 1/4-inch thick chrome-moly motor plate is fitted to the rear of the block. Bolted to it is the large titanium flywheel shield, or bell-housing. Attached to the rear of the bellhousing and wrapped in a ballistic blanket is the reverser. The driveshaft that comes out of the reverser is routed between the driver's legs to the rear axle.

Each Funny Car uses either a four- or five-disc clutch. Here is a five-disc clutch with its four required floater plates. The floater plates are held in alignment by nine large pins. A pressure plate, with 18 fingers, is bolted to these pins.

Behind the engine is a 10.5-inch-diameter clutch with 18 adjustable fingers. The clutch control system is a combination of pneumatic and hydraulic actuators. Unlike a passenger car, which has a single disc, a Funny Car clutch is composed of either four or five discs with floaters in between. The 1999 season saw some competitors switching from the four-disc clutch to the five-disc. "The five-disc is different," says Funny Car driver Ron Capps. "It applies slower and smoother. The four-disc banged the clutch about 3 1/2 seconds into the run and it would kick you in the ass. Because it's so smooth, the run doesn't feel that fast with the five-disc." Clutch management is also controlled by air timers. Too much clutch at the start, and the tires will spin. If the clutch locks up too early, it will drag the engine speed down too low in its power curve. After each run, the clutch is disassembled and new discs and floater plates are installed. Limiting the clutch assembly size is a titanium flywheel shield (bellhousing). The maximum internal depth of the flywheel shield is 9.4 inches. Sandwiched between the flywheel's mounting flange and the rear of the cylinder block is a 1/4-inch-thick motor plate. This plate is manufactured out of 4130 chrome-moly steel and

Neither the front nor the rear of a modern Funny Car is sprung. The front suspension consists of a single A-arm constructed in a triangular fashion from tubing. It is connected to the frame with Heim joints that provide adjustment for wheel alignment. Unlike Top Fuel dragsters, Funny Cars are required to have front brakes. Funny Cars feature aluminum four-piston calipers with slotted discs. The Goodyear 28x5x16 front tires are made specifically for Funny Cars.

is used to secure the engine to the frame. The flywheel shield and motor plate are designed to contain any clutch explosion.

Transmissions are not allowed on a modern Funny Car. Attached to the rear of the flywheel shield is a reverser. A reverser is a small planetary gear set that allows the engine's output to be reversed to the rear axle allowing the car to back up on its own. The driver has a lever in the cockpit that engages and disengages the reverser. A short driveshaft connects to the rear axle, which is limited to a ratio of 3.20. Each end of the driveshaft must have a 360 degree cover of 1/16-inch thick steel or 1/8-inch thick aluminum. This cover is designed to keep the driveshaft from flailing around between the driver's legs in case of a coupler failure.

The Chassis

A Funny Car chassis must be able to take the 4,500 ft-lb torque load of the nitro-burning engine and be stable at over 300 miles per hour. A rigid, well-designed chassis is the secret. Several specialty racing chassis manufacturers supply frames to the race teams. While under the rules a Funny Car chassis may have a wheelbase between 100 and 125 inches, all competitors opt for the longer 125-inch wheelbase. A longer wheelbase car is easier to handle. All frames are constructed out of 4130 chrome-moly tubing and weigh approximately 125 pounds. Mild steel is allowed, but for a frame to be of equal strength, it would be twice as heavy. A chrome-moly frame must be welded by an approved TIG Heliarc process and the welds may not be ground. Each frame must have a manufacturer's name, serial number, and date of manufacture. NHRA inspects each competitor's frames and affixes a sticker prior to competition. In the NHRA rule book, very specific dimensions are indicated for the tubing used in the roll cage that protects the driver. The diameter of the bars that surround the driver must be a minimum of 1 1/2 inches. The surfaces of these bars, which could possibly come into contact with the driver's helmet, must be padded.

A Funny Car does not have a suspension system. The rear axle is solidly mounted to the frame. The tread of the rear tire must not extend outside the body's rear wheel opening and must be within 3 inches of the edge of the rear wheel opening. Up front, the tires must be within 6 inches of the front wheel opening. The front suspension has adjustable A-arms that are also solidly mounted to the frame. This adjustment allows for alignment (caster, camber, and toe-in) to ensure that the car tracks properly at speed. All four wheels are required to have brakes, and large disc units are fitted to each wheel.

Between the engine and driver is an aluminum firewall that is .050 inches thick. In that firewall are two windows in the area of the rear of the valve covers. Called "fire windows" because they allow the driver to see an engine compartment fire, these openings must be covered with laminated safety glass or Lexan. Directly in front of the engine is where the air-actuated timers are located within a carbon fiber box. These timers control clutch application, ignition timing, and fuel management for each run. At the front of the frame is the 19-gallon

The bare Funny Car chassis is compact and extremely rigid. It is constructed from chrome-moly tubing and has a 125-inch wheelbase. The sturdy roll cage completely surrounds the driver. This car is in the process of being assembled for an upcoming race. The horizontally mounted red bottle on the right front of the frame is one of two fire bottles.

The rear axle on a Funny Car is solidly mounted to the frame. NHRA rules dictate a ratio of 3.20:1. Rear brakes have aluminum calipers and a carbon fiber disc. The brake lines are aircraft-quality braided stainless steel. The larger line in the foreground is connected to the lower frame rail and carries the engine's blow-by to the rear mounted catch can.

fuel tank and a three-gallon oil tank. Mounted behind the driver is a catch can more commonly called a "puke tank." It collects the engine's oil blow-by, which is routed from the valve covers through the frame tubing to the tank. Between rounds, the teams will regularly drain the accumulated oil from the lower frame tubes.

Unlike a passenger car, a Funny Car does not have a brake pedal, but a hand-actuated lever to the right of the driver seat. The driver seat is not built for comfort, but safety. It is required to be covered in Nomex and has a five-point driver restraint system. Funny Car drivers do not like a lot of padding in the seat, because it insulates them from the feel of the car. There are only two pedals on the floor of a Funny Car: the clutch and the accelerator. The accelerator pedal will normally have some type of stirrup or arm on the top to retain the driver's foot and allow him to have a positive method of closing the throttle in the event of a problem with a throttle return spring. The steering wheel is formed out of aluminum, in a butterfly shape. Up above the driver's right shoulder is the parachute release.

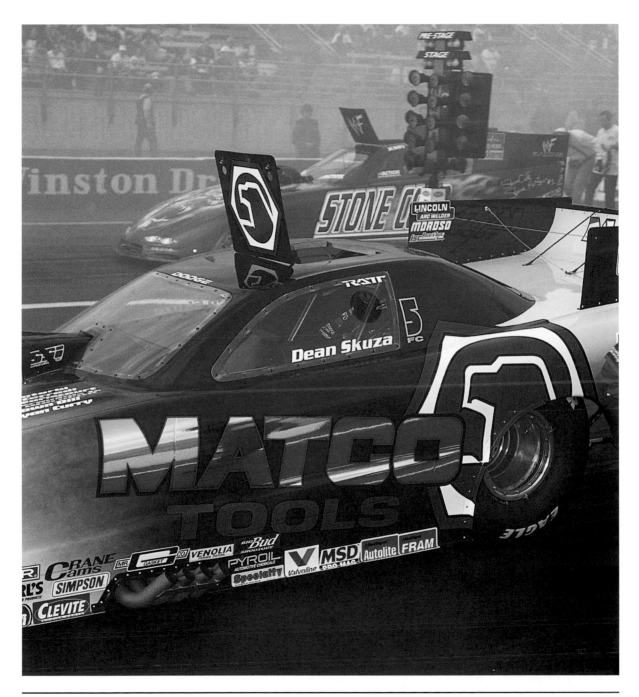

Following long, smoky burnouts, these two Funny Cars are backing up through the lingering haze of their tire smoke. Both drivers have opened their roof escape hatches. This helps to clear the driver's compartment of any accumulated smoke. Funny Cars are required to have an opening in the side glass at least 6 inches in diameter.

The silver can on the back of the frame is the catch can for engine blow-by. It is commonly called a "puke tank" and can have as much as a gallon of oil in it after a run. The silver lines on the ground are shroud lines for the parachutes, which are attached to the frame.

Also in the cockpit is an actuator for the on-board fire bottles. A minimum 20-pound system is mandatory. The system must be divided to provide a minimum of 15 pounds to the engine compartment (with nozzles placed at the front of each set of exhaust headers) and the remaining 5 pounds to the driver's compartment. Also in the driver's compartment is a lever that actuates the fuel pumps,

and an ignition kill switch. If a car is equipped with a two-way radio, there will be switches for its activation. Instrumentation is limited to a single oil pressure gauge or no instrumentation at all. An air bottle is mounted behind the driver. It's connected to the driver's helmet by a hose and provides a constant supply of fresh air to the driver.

For traction, the 16-inch-diameter, 16-inch-wide aluminum rear wheels mount Goodyear drag slicks. These tires are 36 inches in diameter, have an 18-inch-wide tread, and must have a maximum 118-inch circumference when inflated to an operating pressure of 5 pounds. The 16-inch-diameter by 2.5-inch-wide front wheels are also aluminum. They mount specially made tires that can withstand speeds in excess of 300 miles per hour.

If the fuel system is the heart of a Funny Car, the pneumatic timers are the brains. Mounted in a box between the fuel tank and engine is a bank of pneumatic controllers. Funny Cars are not allowed to use any computers or electronic controls to manage the car's fuel, ignition, or clutch management systems. Each of these pneumatic solenoids is set to activate at a certain time into the run and activate a certain system. In all, there may be over 20 timed events within three seconds of the start of the run. Programming these solenoids is a black art that each crew chief practices. Done properly, a Funny Car run will be smooth and fast. Done improperly, an infinite number of things can go wrong.

The Body

Today's Funny Car body has the sleek sexy looks of one of Detroit's latest concept cars. According to the rules, the body must be representative of a 1995 or later two-door mass-produced automobile. Only coupes or sedans are allowed—no convertibles. Seen

This is the 1999 Z-28 Camaro Funny Car that Ron Capps drove for Don Prudhomme. Funny Car bodies are required to be based on a production vehicle no more than five years old. Certain liberties are taken with the shape of the car. Tops may be chopped a maximum of 2 inches and the bodies may be lengthened or shortened. All Funny Car bodies are constructed of carbon fiber composites.

competing today are Chevrolet Camaro and Corvette, Pontiac Firebird, Ford Mustang, or Dodge Avenger. For light weight and strength, all of today's top competitors' bodies are built from a special four-element carbon fiber weave. The total body weight is 250 pounds.

The minimum body width is 60 inches, and maximum variance in width from front to rear is 6 inches. The body may be lengthened or shortened, but the front and rear contour must resemble the design and contours of the specific production car it is built to resemble. One-inch fender flares are permitted on the forward half of the front and rear wheel openings. Enclosing the wheel openings is not permitted. In the rear, two hinged doors are allowed, with a maximum

of 100 square inches per side, to vent air at the rear of the car. No other openings to let air in or out are allowed. Also in the rear are the two parachutes. Dual parachutes are an NHRA requirement and each must have its own release cable. While the parachutes are mounted on the body, the shroud lines are attached to the chassis.

A Funny Car roof may be chopped a maximum of 2 inches. Minimum roof width is 32 inches, and the length must be within 4 inches of the car on which the body is based. A working escape hatch is required in the roof. It must be a minimum of 17 by 18 inches and hinged in the front. A release mechanism that can open the hatch from either the outside or inside keeps the door secure at speed. Without the support crew available to open

Funny Car teams will occasionally visit the wind tunnel for a check of the car's aerodynamics. Minor changes will often result in a competitive edge at 300 miles per hour. Here the Kendall Oil Camaro Z-28 Funny Car gets a quick trip through the GM wind tunnel. Charles Krasner/JVS Enterprises

Prior to a run, three or four of the crew members will move the body from its support cradle and place it on the chassis. The twin parachutes are attached to the rear of the body with shroud lines that connect to the frame.

The square outline on the hood of John Force's Castrol Mustang Funny Car is the burst panel required by NHRA rules. In case of an engine explosion, it allows the pressure to be vented through this panel, preventing the body from blowing off. Behind the burst panel is the injector with its three circular butterflies. The small squares on the body surface are where the body's tubular framework attaches.

the body at the end of the track following a run, the driver exits the through this hatch. While hood scoops are not allowed, an opening for the injectors is required. In front of the injector opening, a 288-square-inch burst panel is required on the hood. A burst panel, attached to the body with plastic screws, is a safety valve that will blow free, venting the underside of the body in case of an engine or supercharger explosion. It is designed to blow out, reducing the likelihood of spectacularly separating the body from the frame.

A windshield is mandatory on a modern Funny Car and must be installed within three degrees of the angle of installation on the car on which it is based. Clear side windows are optional, and most competitors have them installed. Side windows are required to have a 6-inch opening adjacent to the driver. This is a safety requirement that would allow a safety crew's fire extinguisher nozzle to flood the interior. A clear rear window is not required, but a facsimile must be painted on the body.

Both of these Funny Cars are Pontiac Firebirds. Rules allow the addition of a spoiler to the rear deck. This rear deck spoiler is more of a shelf than an actual wing. It is restricted to a maximum width of 54 inches, and spill plates frame the outer edges. This rear spoiler can generate up to 5,000 pounds of downforce. Funny Cars are forbidden to have ground effect devices.

Spoilers are allowed on a Funny Car body. Up front, they are built into the body; in the rear, a large spoiler is added to the rear deck. This rear deck spoiler is restricted to a maximum width of 54 inches. Its trailing edge may not extend more than 56 inches past the centerline of the rear axle. The design is restricted to more of a large shelf than an actual wing with a leading and trailing edge. Spill plates frame the outer edges of the rear spoiler. These plates can be as high as 5 inches above the roof line. Adjustments or movement of the rear spoiler is not allowed

during the run. A Funny Car's rear spoiler can generate up to 5,000 pounds of downforce to the rear tires. Ground effect devices are strictly forbidden on Funny Cars.

To purchase everything needed to build one Funny Car, you'll need at least $200,000 (see sidebar). This does not include spare parts, a transporter to move it, or the support crew to service it. By comparison, a Winston Cup NASCAR race car costs approximately $75,000. But that NASCAR racer runs more than 100 miles per hour slower than the Funny Car.

A Funny Car driver must have quick reaction time. Dean Skuza, driver of the Matco Tools Funny Car, is one of the best, with an average reaction time of 0.497 seconds (a perfect reaction time is 0.400). Here, at the 1999 Winston Finals, he has hit the throttle for his first qualifying run. Flames from the headers shoot over the roof, as the engine is instantly spooling up to more than 8,000 rpm.

RACING A FUNNY CAR

Starting with the Winternationals in February, and then about every other week throughout the racing season, there is an NHRA national event at which Funny Cars run. This is what the sponsors pay the teams to do, and this is why the fans come out. Most national events are three-day affairs, with qualifying on Friday and Saturday and eliminations on Sunday. A few are four-day events, with qualifying beginning on Thursday. Each team gets only four chances to qualify to race on Sunday. At each national event there are only 16 spots available on the Funny Car race ladder. There are no provisionals; everyone must qualify—even the previous year's champion. And everyone must be ready to race—no excuses. Nobody will postpone the race because one of the teams isn't ready. Drag racing

is one of the most unpredictable of motorsports events. There have been national events where top teams have failed to qualify and others where a virtual unknown has beaten the best.

When a Funny Car team unloads the car at the track, it is not completely ready to run. The engine will be mocked-up, with the heads and blower placed on the engine, but not fully bolted down. This gives the crew chief the flexibility to change components that will determine the tune-up prior to the first qualifying run.

The crew chief decides on the car's tune-up for each run. Many factors are taken into consideration—most important are weather and track condition. A seemingly minor temperature or humidity change will dramatically affect how a car will run. Each race track has its own

Prior to making a run, the Funny Car crew chief is responsible for the tune-up that will produce the most power and maintain traction throughout the quarter-mile. NHRA restricts the use of electronic devices to control any of the car's clutch management, fuel management, or timing adjustments during the run. These functions are controlled by pneumatic controllers mounted between the fuel tank and engine.

personality. Some tracks have better traction in certain areas and the crew chief must tune the car to take advantage of the adhesion. It's not unusual to see a Funny Car make a perfect run for two-thirds of the track, lose traction at the top end, and start spinning the tires through the traps. The car must be tuned to run the entire quarter-mile.

About one hour prior to making a run (qualifying or competition), each Funny Car team will start its car in the pits. The car, minus the body, will be securely up off the ground on stands alongside its transporter. The driver sits in the car. He and members of the pit crew wear gas masks for this procedure. The starter is plugged in and the car is started. This is a shakedown to be sure everything is race-ready. The engine runs at an idle, while the crew checks for any leaks. These cars run rich at idle and the fumes from the nitromethane fuel are pungent—that's why gas masks are required. One good snoot full has the same effect as tear gas: watery eyes, running nose, and a loss of breath. In addition to the fumes, the thunder from the headers is apocalyptic.

Prior to making a run, the car's engine is started in the pits to set the ignition timing and check for oil or fuel leaks. This crewman is fitting the starter to the blower's snout. On top of the injector hat is a tool tray filled with specific tools needed for the tune-up.

The Castrol Syntec Funny Car has just been fired up in the pits and the starter motor has just been removed. The crewman on the right is continuing to squirt gasoline into the injector while he uses his left hand to turn on the fuel pump. Gas masks are required because of the noxious fumes produced by the nitromethane fuel.

Everyone on John Force's Castrol team has a role to play when the car is fired up in the pits. Force is in the driver seat while his "brain trust" of Austin Coil and Bernie Fedderly (in white shirts) are making the final adjustments to the engine. Other crew members are visually checking for leaks or any other potential problems. In the background, race fans have gathered to smell the nitro fumes and listen to the sound of the engine. Once the engine is shut down, the oil and spark plugs will be changed.

This is why the driver and crew also wear ear protection. When a Funny Car is fired in the pits, it draws fans like a fight in a school yard. Everyone gathers around to be close to the action. As soon as those closest get a good nose full of nitro fumes, they quickly retreat. For most drag-race fans, the smell of nitro is an aphrodisiac.

A secondary purpose for starting the car is to "burn in" the clutch. The driver firmly holds the brake handle (to keep the rear tires from turning) and lets out the clutch pedal. The engine will not stall when the clutch is engaged, because it is designed to slip. Once engaged with the brake held firmly, the driver will quickly—very quickly—stab the throttle once or twice. This is done to allow all of the clutch components to seat properly. When machined, each of the components has microscopic high and low spots. This burning-in process evens out all of the clutch components' surfaces and makes the clutch more responsive and predictable.

The call has been made bringing all Funny Cars to the staging lanes. Each car is towed by a support vehicle that carries the electric starter, crews, and any tools needed for final adjustments. This is the calm before the storm, when drivers and crew members get a chance to swap lies with each other.

Once the engine is shut down, the oil is drained and replaced and the spark plugs are changed. When called by track officials, the cars will be towed into the staging lanes to await their designated time to run. Each driver has his own preference as to when he gets in the car or what he does prior to the run.

"I usually listen to some good music," says Matco Tools Funny Car driver Dean Skuza. "If we're one of the last pairs of Funny Cars to run, I'll go up to the line and watch to see what's going on. I try to get in when the fourth car ahead of me fires up. I'd rather get in earlier than later, even if it's hot out. I can sit in there and relax and get in the car tighter that way." Once in the car, drivers continue to tighten their seat belts. "Everything kind of settles in and you can keep tightening the belts. I like to sit in really tight so I can feel the car better. The closer you are to anything, the better you can feel the vibrations," says Skuza.

Sitting in the car ready to race is where the drivers want to be. They are not

When the cars hit the staging lanes, they are race-ready. Ballistic blankets are in place over the valve covers to reduce flying shrapnel in case of an explosion. The car on the left has covers over the fuel tank and rear tire to prevent changes due to heat.

distracted by fans or TV crews and this time alone allows them to become one with the car. "I usually run through in my mind what to do if something goes wrong—if it blows a tire or catches on fire," says U.S. Tobacco Funny Car driver Ron Capps. "Then I start walking through a run in my mind. Hit the throttle, pedal it, and walk it through in my mind." Capps also stays focused on the job at hand. "I don't let little stuff bug me. A lot of drivers get really irritated with little things. I think that works against them."

For qualifications, the pairings of cars and lane choices are determined by NHRA officials. For the first round of eliminations, the pairings are done by qualification times (the quickest ETs run against the slower ETs) and lane choice goes to the car with the lowest elapsed time of the pair. In subsequent rounds of competition, lane choice continues to go to the car that ran the quicker ET. Lane choice is subjective. The crew chief, and occasionally the driver, will check out the track prior to their run. They want the side of

Once the driver is given the signal by his crew, he will roll forward through what was once known as the "bleach box." This area behind the starting line is kept watered down. The tires will spin more easily if they are wet. With a clear track ahead, the driver will press down on the accelerator. The engine will rev to approximately 5,000 rpm, and the rear wheels will start to spin. A stop on the linkage keeps the throttle from opening all but a few degrees. Without that stop, the engine would overrev and self-destruct.

These two cars are about to be pulled out onto the track for their run. The drivers, hidden behind the bodies, are snugly belted in place thinking about their upcoming five-second 300-mile per hour ride. The crews are thinking about their responsibilities to get the car started and ready to race.

the track with the best racing "groove." The groove is established by each competitor that has laid down a coat of rubber on the track. "There is a look and a feel and you pick the best spot," says Force's head crew chief, Austin Coil. "Generally the condition is dependent upon how the rubber is adhering to the race track. The rubber sticks and sticks and sticks and the next time—it tears some off and throws it away." Often, during the burnout, some of the rubber on the track will peel away,

exposing the concrete or asphalt. "You don't want to find a bald spot when you stage the car, if the burnout peeled the rubber up," says Coil. "For the run, you need to move the car over to where it isn't peeled up."

When next in line to run, the car is towed into place, facing down the track, with the support vehicle alongside and the starter motor attached to the front of the supercharger. When the track starter signals, the magnetos are switched on and

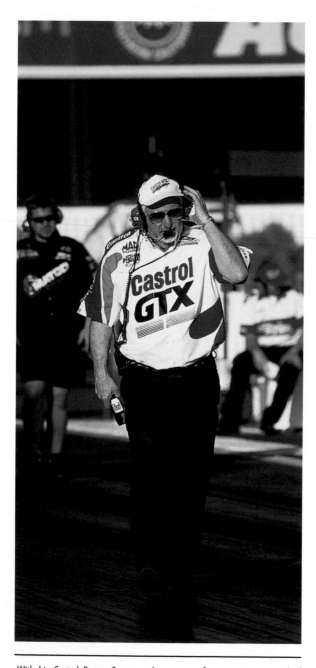

With his Castrol Funny Car several cars away from running, crew chief Bernie Fedderly takes a quick walk out to the track. In his right hand is a temperature sensing gun that is used to take the temperature of the racing surface. The headset keeps him in constant communication with Castrol head crew chief Austin Coil and driver John Force.

the starter motor begins to spin the engine. One of the crew uses a small squirt bottle to spray gasoline into the injector butterflies. Gasoline is used because it will light off easily in the cylinders and get the engine up to speed. With the engine running, the body will be closed and the driver will roll forward through the water box for the burnout.

The burnout is one of the highlights of any Funny Car run. Technically it's done to get the slicks up to operating temperature and to lay rubber on the track to improve the racing groove. To commence the burnout, the driver rolls through a water box and then hits the throttle, lighting up the tires. All Funny Car drivers do them, but Force and Skuza work in tire smoke the way van Gogh worked in oils. They have finessed the burnout into a classic art form, doing the longest of any of the drivers. Both have been known to extend their burnouts for three-fourths of the track. "I do long burnouts because it looks cool," says Skuza with a big grin. "That's the only reason—it's the showmanship part of it—people love it, man." Skuza's love of lengthy burnouts surfaced at Norwalk, Ohio, in a match race. His burnout extended through the traps at the end of the quarter-mile. While backing up from that burnout, Skuza could hear the crowd cheering over the noise of the engine—something not typically audible inside a running Funny Car.

Following the burnout, the driver will push in the clutch and reach down and engage the reverser. This allows the car to back up. When the driver starts backing, he will use what little vision he has to the front and sides to keep the car in the center of the lane. Once he gets within 200 feet of

The signal has been given for the Interstate Batteries Funny Car team to fire up the engine. The driver switches on the ignition, while one crew member handles the starter and another the fuel bottle. Once the engine is started and running properly, the body will be closed for the burnout.

The burnout is done to add rubber to the track, improving the racing surface and to heat the rear tires for better adhesion. Approximately four gallons of fuel are used during the burnout.

the starting line, the crew chief, or one of the designated crew members, will guide him the rest of the way back, using hand signals. The car is positioned slightly behind the starting line where the driver holds the brake and disengages the reverser. At this time, the body is opened and final adjustments are made. A crew member will reach in and reset the clutch and another will purge the solenoid system of any air. Some crew chiefs use this time to make a final adjustment to the engine. All crew members are visually checking for any leaks or anything mechanical that could be a potential problem. Some teams do not open the body; instead, the driver will make the clutch

and solenoid adjustments. The last thing to do is to remove the throttle stop on the injector linkage. This stop, attached for the burnout, limits the throttle opening to a few degrees, restricting the engine's rpm to 5,500.

With adjustments completed and the body closed, the driver must get the car staged. Once again, a crew member or the crew chief will assist the driver in positioning the car, stopping him about 10 inches from the prestage beam. It's then up to the driver to roll ahead into the beams. Once fully staged, the driver will do what is called "doubling up." This is when he manually turns on all the fuel pumps. At track side, a slight decrease in

Following the burnout, the driver will stop the car and engage the reverser to back up to the starting line. While backing, one of the crew will move into the driver's line of sight to help him position the car in the best location on the starting line. Here the crewman in front is relaying the direction signal he is getting from the crew chief in the background. The roof hatch on the Kendall Camaro is open to help vent the inside of any residual tire smoke.

Once the car is stopped following the burnout, the body is opened and the clutch is reset. The stop that limited the throttle opening is removed and a final check is made to see that everything on the car is ready to run 300 miles per hour. The body is closed and the roof hatch is double checked.

Head crew chief for the Castrol Funny Car, Austin Coil, has stopped John Force a few feet short of the staging lights. Coil looks into the car and gives Force the "OK" sign to let him know everything is ready. From this point, Force will inch the car forward to illuminate the "prestage" light and then the "stage light."

engine rpm is noticed. Once the car is staged and waiting to run, the engine idles at 2,400 to 2,500 rpm. It's ready to go.

Sitting at the starting line waiting for the tree, the driver's senses are peaked. "The concentration is unbelievable," says Skuza. "If anyone could concentrate like that whenever they wanted, they could do anything. It's a cool thing, I get off on that feeling of concentration. It's almost like you can melt something with your eyes—like a laser beam. You're completely removed from everything but the task at hand. I wish I could put myself into that

type of concentration anytime I wanted. There's no way to duplicate that or simulate that feeling. It's pure adrenaline that puts you into that state."

Funny Cars run on what is called a "pro tree." This means that the Christmas tree's yellow lights flash, and then 0.4 seconds later, the green light illuminates. If the driver waits until the green light flashes, he will be late. He must react with the yellow and push the accelerator pedal to the floor. Within a fraction of a second, the engine spins to 8,000 rpm. In less than one second, the car has accelerated

When the driver hits the throttle, the sides of the large rear slicks distort, as the tread grips the track. The slicks flatten out, placing a footprint on the track as long as it is wide. The distortion of the tire makes the rear of the car squat down.

to 100 miles per hour. Beginning at about 0.8 second into the run, the distributor will be retarded, dropping the engine's rpm to 7,500. This timing retard will last until 1.3 seconds into the run. (That time, between 0.8 and 1.3 seconds, is a crucial time where the rear tires tend to shake.) The rear tires are in a transition state, going from the flat large tread that they have while sitting at rest, to a state where they are more round, aided by centrifugal force. The tire is trying to straighten up. One second into the run, the engine speed is at 7,500 rpm, but the driveshaft is turning only 2,800 rpm. This difference is the clutch slippage.

The first 1.3 seconds of the run is crucial. If everything works perfectly, all the driver needs to do is aim the car and hold on. Or, the car's tires can go up in smoke or shake. The crew chief's job is to set the application of clutch, fuel, and timing, so the car transitions through this time period smoothly.

"You have to get through the dreaded 1.3, or early part of the run, because if you try and make it move too early, it just smokes the tires," says Skuza's crew chief, Lance Larsen. "One-point-three seconds, that's the instant where it tries to stand the tire up. When they leave, they will squat and go out a little way and raise up. If you try to raise them up too fast you lose the tire footprint and it will shake. It will shake because it's [the engine] too lean, it will shake because it has too much

When coming off the starting line in a Funny Car, if everything is working correctly, there is no finesse with the throttle—it's simply stab it and steer. Here, Ron Capps, the driver of the U.S. Tobacco Funny Car, has just left the line and is on his way to a good run. The force from the acceleration reaches as high as five g-forces, as the car continues to accelerate.

[power], it will shake because it has too little [power]—it will shake for a lot of different reasons. It's a complex problem. If I knew everything about it, I'd never shake the tires." Shaking the tires on a Funny Car is abusive to the driver. When the tires shake, there is so much violent movement that the driver cannot see the track ahead and will exit the car with a headache. "No shake, no rattle is like driving a car at 55 miles an hour—it's that controllable," says Skuza. "You really enjoy those runs."

The other problem encountered at the start is smoking the rear tires. This is usually caused by applying too much power, too soon. If the tires go up in smoke, the driver can only hope his competitor's car is also smoking its tires. Good Funny Car drivers have learned the art of "pedaling," or lifting off the throttle momentarily to stop wheel spin or tire shake. It's an art that only a few of the top drivers have perfected. "Sometimes," says Skuza, "I'll know before it's going to happen, and I'll give it what Lance [crew chief Larsen] calls a 'courtesy slap.' I pedal it for no reason, because I think it's going to be a problem. It only takes a few hundredths. We've run as quick as 4.89 doing that."

A quick reaction to the starting lights can be the difference between winning and losing. A fast shutter speed caught this difference. The driver of the Pioneer Funny Car, in the background, has stepped on the throttle and is on his way, while the Kenworth-sponsored car, in the foreground, has yet to hit the throttle.

With flames streaming back from the headers, the car in the far lane has just crossed the finish line, a scant few feet ahead of the car in the near lane. Unfortunately, the car in the near lane has just blown up and has flames streaming from its underside. ©Joe Veraldi

OFFICIAL STARTER—
THE ONE WHO TURNS 'EM LOOSE

At each NHRA national event, there is one man who runs the on-track show—the NHRA's official starter, Rick Stewart. Stewart is no newcomer to drag racing. In the 1960s, he successfully raced fuel dragsters. He also spent 15 years as the back-up to the original NHRA starter, Buster Couch.

Stewart's job is to unleash the beasts. He's the one who pushes the button to activate the starting lights. But it's not as simple as that. A bigger part of his job is safety—safety for the drivers, fans, and crew. "Safety is the biggest part of my responsibility," says Stewart. Safety is followed closely by the need to provide a level playing field for all competitors. "Drag racing is pretty simple—reaction time and car performance. The starter doesn't want to be involved. If I have to get involved, that's when I get upset. But that doesn't occur very often. It should be driver reaction time and car performance—end of story."

On the day of eliminations, it's Stewart who gives the signal to the crews to start the engines. This is done after he checks, by radio, with race control up in the tower to see if the track is clear of any debris or oil. When the cars pull into the water box for the burnout, he starts a stopwatch that he keeps around his neck. The stopwatch is to record how long the cars' engines are running. Stewart allows 85 to 90 seconds to elapse from the time the burnout commences to the time the cars are staged. "That way, if a guy has a little problem, I know exactly how much time is left for them to get it resolved." If one of the cars has a problem and is not ready to go, the race starts without him .

When the cars are on the track, Stewart and his assistants are constantly looking over each car to make sure it's safe to race. "I have a mental program I go through with each car," says Stewart. "I'm looking for oil leaks, fuel leaks, safety equipment on the driver, including neck collar, seat belts, shoulder harnesses, gloves, and arm restraints. I make sure the pins are out of the chute pack, that all the tires have air, that the body is latched down properly, and that the top hatch is locked down. I have starting line people working with me who are real experienced guys. They're an extra set of eyes on the outside. If they see something, they point it out to me and we look at it." If something is spotted by one of his crew, such as a fuel or oil leak, it will be pointed out with exaggerated hand gestures. The final responsibility rests on Stewart's shoulders—he's the only one who can give the signal for a driver to shut his engine off.

Because of the costs involved, the importance of safety, and the level of professionalism among the drivers, amateur starting line games are not played in the Funny Car class. At the starting line, Stewart makes eye contact with the drivers. "I give them a smile and a thumbs-up to give them that last second to relax. I want them to concentrate on the starting line, getting a

The man in the red-and-white NHRA shirt wearing the straw hat is Rick Stewart, NHRA's official starter. Here, he's getting ready to send two of the sport's top drivers on another run. As soon as Ron Capps in the U.S. Copenhagen /U.S. Tobacco car in the foreground stages, Stewart will cut them loose.

good reaction time, and getting down the race track safely and straight." Once Stewart is convinced that both cars are safe to race and the track is clear, he will activate the starting lights and hold onto his hat as the cars burst off the starting line and rocket down the track.

The noise at the starting line between two fuel-burning Funny Cars is unbelievable.

Stewart wears specially molded earplugs to attenuate the noise. "It's like having your head inside a jet engine when the afterburner is ignited," says Stewart with a grin. "It's an unbelievable experience. As many times as I've been up there, it still amazes me to have 5,000-plus horsepower in each lane accelerating to 100 miles per hour in less than one second."

Tony Pedregon remembers the first time he successfully pedaled his Funny Car.

I was racing Al Hoffman. When the car left and it was just on the edge, it started to rattle a tire. Something inside of me said to pedal it, and my foot did it automatically. Just everything happened where I got out of the throttle and I just got back on it. I was expecting the car to get sideways and go up in smoke, but I wanted to chase him down. The thing hooked up and carried the front end—it just blew me away. I saw Al's fender and I really thought I could catch him. I lost the race, but when I got out of the car the crew came up and said they couldn't believe it, they saw smoke coming off the tires.

When you see white smoke off the tires, it's usually good night. You lose traction and so much fuel gets poured into the engine that it makes a whole lot more horsepower and it's over. Every time I'd tried pedaling in the past—and not caught it in time—the car would go right back into smoke, because you don't let the rpm settle down. You don't let the tire get flat again. To me, it's an art when you see a driver do that—it's an art to have that kind of throttle control. What helped me more than anything was doing match races on junk tracks. John [Force] took me to a bunch of those in 1996, where I actually got on a bad surface and had to try different things.

We have this old 8-millimeter movie that my brother and I studied. It was when Beadle, the Snake, and Lombardo were "the guys." John was driving the Wendy's Corvette. He'd qualify, but was not competitive. But he was always the guy you wanted to see because he could talk. We were amazed by watching John's run—he pedaled it. He's doing the same thing today! And they wonder why he's so good!

(John Force is the most experienced Funny Car driver on the circuit. He was pedaling a Funny Car when many of his competitors were still in diapers.)

Ron Capps describes his relationship to the car this way:

On a good run, at about two seconds into the run, it starts applying the clutch and it really starts truckin.' Everything starts going by like you're in hyperspace. Everything but where you're looking goes whoosh. It's an amazing feeling. Once you're out there past half-track, you want to keep your hands on the wheel. You're just trying to focus on one spot way out there. You really have to concentrate. If the car wants to make a move, I'll try to get it right back. You have to stay on top of it, because in these cars, if you let them go too far—they'll own you.

After half-track, when it's haulin' ass, I know everything is cool and I can see the finish line way up there, and I'll get my hand on the parachute lever. I'll hit it when I'm still pretty far out there. Because of the car's speed, I can still see the scoreboard (at the finish line) when I hit the chutes. I've always been taught to hit the chutes early, because when something happens down there, the thing that is going to save you is the chute. I've got it timed, I'll hit it, drive right to the finish line, lift, and right then the chute blossoms.

The driver experiences minus five g-forces as the chutes blossom and start to slow the car.

Another problem a driver may face during a run is when the engine "drops a cylinder." In the simplest of terms, dropping a cylinder means that the fire goes out in one of the eight cylinders. Instead of running on all eight, the engine is running on seven cylinders and down approximately 1,000 horsepower. The result is a disproportionate amount of exhaust from the headers. Because the headers are angled slightly to the side, the differential in exhaust gas pressure will push the car toward the side of the track where the cylinder is out.

"If it's out at the hit, you really don't have any way of knowing it, unless it pushes you to the side, because they still run pretty good to the 60-foot mark," says Capps. "If it puts a cylinder out any time after that, a half-second or a second, you'll hear the motor change, and it will kind of move you a little bit. If it puts it out way out there, usually I can hear it first, the tone changes just a tiny bit, and then I know something's happening here." Regarding dropping a cylinder during a run, Dean Skuza says, "I can feel it especially if it drops one early. I can almost tell you which one, whether it's 1, 3, 5, or 7. I can tell 5 or 7 just by the way it moves the car and the way it rattles the motor. You get to that point when you're running one engine combination for a long period of time."

Fans love to watch Funny Cars running at night. When the cars leave the starting line, it's as if Elvis walked in and all the flash bulbs started popping in the stands. The show is made even more spectacular by the flames shooting 6 feet out of the headers, something not fully visible in daylight.

"I love it at night," exclaims Skuza. "Not only speaking as a driver, but as fan. When I was a kid, everyone wanted to see the Funny Cars run at night—I think all drag racing should be at night. It's so much of a spectacle." Capps agrees, "Night is pretty cool. From a driving standpoint, it reminds me of the old match race days. When you hit the throttle on a Funny Car, it lights everything up around you for the first 40 or 50 feet. You can see the flames out the window a bit and then the car starts accelerating; you can watch them disappear from the window. That's what's cool about the night racing!" Pedregon finds night racing a little more challenging. "At night it gets a little distracting, because of the balls of fire out there."

When a race is televised, the production crew will always have an announcer at the end of the track to get a quick interview with the winner. They try to get the driver's perspective on the previous five seconds of racing. Tony Pedregon comments on the relationship between racing and the media:

There's nothing like a good drag race when, at about 1,100 feet, the other guy is right next to you. Today, these things are shooting flames and mixing cylinders and an occasional part flying off of it and it's tough—a lot of times that's the toughest race, because you don't know who won. After the race is over, for a good 15 or 20 seconds, you still don't know who won, even with a radio, because of the amount of static. Usually the camera crew will be the first indication. If there's any question who won, they'll answer it awful quick. If you think you won and the cameras are going to the next guy, you'd better guess again. That's an awful feeling."

Pedregon was lucky enough to fly with the U.S. Navy's Blue Angels. Following a high-speed low level pass, the pilot pulled the fighter into a straight vertical climb. On the radio the pilot anxiously asked Pedregon, "How was that? How does that compare to a Funny Car?"

"Well, it doesn't," replied Pedregon. "I think he was trying to impress me." Pedregon admitted that flying in an F-18 was an interesting, once-in-a-lifetime experience. He stayed up the full 45 minutes, even though he got sick three times. "I can honestly say that ride was like nothing I've ever experienced, but it doesn't compare to a Funny Car." Pedregon adds:

To me driving a Funny Car is like being shot out of a cannon. There are no shocks or air suspension, the tires are the only cushion. During the run, you're so caught up in what the car's doing, you can't enjoy it. You can enjoy it before or after. If it was a good run—you can definitely enjoy it after. It always takes me a little while to know what the car did on the run. During the trip from the finish line to the pits, John Medlin [Pedregon's crew chief] wants feedback and I have to tell him to give me a second. It takes a while before it comes back to me. During the run, the driver's not having fun like on a ride at Disneyland. You don't just sit back and enjoy the ride—it's like riding a bull.

With side-by-side competition, Funny Car drivers are very busy in the five-second time span of the run. The difference between winning and losing can be as little as 0.001 second. Pedregon says,

It all happens so fast, that if you're not paying attention and focusing on what your car is doing and your car drifts out four or five feet—all of a sudden you're out of the groove. The engine is making so much power and because you're not where you want to be, it's starting to rev up and you're spinning the tires. Within that fraction of a second, you see the car in the other lane. Now you're in trouble because you're watching him while he was paying attention to his own car. That's the fine line—the good and the bad in five seconds. Being collected, experienced, and focused—that's the difference between a good driver and a bad driver.

Funny Car drivers rarely get to see these cars at speed at the finish line, except from the driver seat, where mentally they have altered time and space. "It really wakes you up when you're towing back and you see two cars whistling down at 300," says Tony Pedregon. "I've thought, my God, that guy has no control—he's on a bullet with no control. When you're in the car, you feel like you have some control, but when you look at it at the finish line—these are scary machines." John Force looks at it very pragmatically. "We're not fearless, we're all afraid. We've just learned to maintain it!"

94

Once back in the pits after a run, the Funny Car's engine is completely disassembled and rebuilt. Working at a frantic pace, the crew rebuilds the car within 45 minutes. This crewman for the Copenhagen/U.S. Tobacco team is about to refit the pistons to the block, while others are working on the heads and clutch.

INDEX